AND JESUS DAN

The true story of the Milltown Brothers

NIGEL WOOD

M^CNIDDER | & GRACE

Published by McNidder & Grace
Jedburgh
Scotland
United Kingdom

www.mcnidderandgrace.com

First published 2025
© Nigel Wood

The author and publisher would like to thank all copyright holders for permission to reproduce their work. Every effort has been made to obtain necessary permission with reference to copyright material. The publisher apologises if, inadvertently, any sources remain unacknowledged and will be glad to be notified of any corrections that should be incorporated in future editions of the book.

A catalogue record for this work is available from the British Library.

ISBN   9780857162892
eISBN 9780857162908

Cover design by Tabitha Palmer
Front cover photo by Tim Paton and back cover photo by Eve Bibby
Designer: JS Typesetting Ltd, Porthcawl, Wales
Printed and bound in the United Kingdom by Short Run Press, Exeter

For Sarah, the only sister of Mark, Simon and Matthew Nelson.

'She was kind, sweet, vulnerable, loyal, classy, charming, a bit dippy in a good way, hard-working, honest, just a lovely person.'

In October 2021 after a struggle with breast cancer she died peacefully in Colne, Lancashire, aged 55. All of her brothers were with her.

AND JESUS DANCED (TWICE)

William Jellett was born in Dorset in June 1948. He started going to festivals and gigs all over London in the late 1960s and never really stopped, other than an interlude during the 1990s. He was also a regular at Speaker's Corner.

One day on the Tube it struck him he could be the second coming of Jesus and had just never realised it. The name – if not the notion – stuck with fellow music fans.

And if Jesus liked the band, he danced like crazy. Occasionally naked, on stage and if it was really good, he played tambourine or the maracas.

He was a five-star review in human form. In 1974 *NME* dedicated a full-page article to him.

He saw the Milltown Brothers play at the Marquee in 1988, only their sixteenth gig. He danced like merry hell and gave his tambourine some hammer.

He returned to see them again 16 years later at the Borderline in 2004 and he danced like merry hell again.

William died aged 72 in January 2021. His ashes were scattered at Speakers' Corner.

CONTENTS

PROLOGUE

It was a gloriously sunny day. Ignoring the warning from his father Daedalus, Icarus used the wings he made for him to escape from the Labyrinth to do much more than was strictly necessary. Rather than simply making his getaway from the Minotaur, he discovered he loved the experience of freedom and flight. He began to fly for the sheer pleasure and became lost in the ecstasy and enjoyment of the moment. He found he could soar. And soar and swoop he did. Higher and higher. Such that he flew way too high, too close to the sun. It melted the wax holding his wings together, and he fell to earth.

The story is one of the most abiding and well known from Greek mythology. It would be good to think it is because we are all too aware of our weaknesses and frailties. The dangers inherent in particularly – but not exclusively – an excess of the male ego. The sheer joy of it all. Getting lost in what's going on. Taking life for granted. Such that we don't think at all. Or if we do, we may feel a tiny bit invincible. In control.

But we're not, are we?

We always have to be lucky too. All the time.

INTRODUCTION

Way back when in 2004 I reluctantly met a pale, slightly out of shape, fair-haired bloke called Matthew Nelson, his name meant nothing to me, despite having a handful of Milltown Brothers' songs on my iPod.

I was that kind of half-arsed music fan at the time. Growing family. Crazy job. DIY. Not enough seeing bands. That gap in-between being young, madly into it and old, madly into it.

He looked about 40, was strangely charming and had the gentle aura of a slightly world-weary, mild-mannered cherub. This was some 15 years after Mandy James had described him as *'a sultry Botticelli angel'* in her review of the Milltown Brothers' gig at Manchester Boardwalk in *NME*, November 1989.

He wasn't what I'd been expecting, I'd been expecting a dickhead. And I certainly had no idea I wasn't the first person to make the cherub or dickhead associations, including the man himself.

"'That's just behind our house!" explains Matt, the boy I called an "angry cherub" in a review, causing him to worry about his weight. "Cherubs are fat, aren't they?" he asked.' Andrew Collins, 'Bed of Roses', *NME*, May 1989.

'You're a dickhead.' Anonymous girl at Manchester Poly to Matthew on his return from a summer playing with the Word Association in the south of France, October 1987.

'We're either portrayed as drunken dickheads or boring old farts. At this moment I happen to be drunk and it's up to everyone else to decide whether I'm a dickhead.' Matthew with Iestyn George, 'Burn Baby Burnley', *NME*, August 1991.

When I say I reluctantly met Matthew, it's because I was being forced to work with him. I was making a couple of TV sponsorship films for the Co-operative Bank and was expecting – as was the norm – to appoint my own tried, tested and friendly film production team to do so.

But the Bank did things a little differently. Granada TV was ITV's regional franchise in the north-west – *Coronation Street*, Tony Wilson… Jeremy Kyle on the rise – and one of the Bank's key media partners.

Unfortunately for me, this meant I was obliged to use their in-house film production people. And Matthew was going to be my contact. I wasn't looking forward to our first meeting, and neither was he. I couldn't be bothered to get to know him and didn't want to work with him.

I liked him instantly, finding him strangely charming. I couldn't help it, and it says much about him that he never held my soon confessed preconceptions against me.

As does the fact he didn't fill me in for ages about the link between him and my iPod. Not that he knew about my iPod, but you know. And even then it took a ridiculously rainy day in Blackpool for that to happen. It stopped us filming and I was running out of things to say in Wetherspoons. *'Have you always done this kind of work?'*

He paused for a few seconds, looking at me, then talked about his past in the most diffident, reticent and humble way you can imagine. Maybe it was still a bit raw, ten years on; I didn't realise he was only three years out of what he now calls his seven-year recovery plan. Which was no plan at all, it had just taken that long. Said he'd been in this little band, they'd released a couple of albums. One had done okay. I had to ask him what they were called and delighted in pulling out my iPod and showing him his songs when he told me.

Typical as it is of him, such modesty is difficult to comprehend when looking at some of the boy's press interviews from years earlier – as the 'Burn Baby Burnley' *NME* article from 1991 amply demonstrates: 'We piss on so many other bands. I know we do. I have no peers on the current music scene.'

Matthew concurs: '*Oh dear, it's not easy pretending to be a rock star, I really should have been kept well away from the press.*'

Twenty years later I started working on the idea for this book with the Milltown Brothers. It had been kicking around in my mind for years, a morality tale about a band that could have been huge, were about to be so and somehow managed to avoid it. And in their case leave Oasis, Blur, Pulp and the rest to the success those bands thoroughly deserved... as much as anyone does.

I'd become – and still am – mildly obsessed with how life is just an infinitesimal number of slender slices of luck from start to finish. At every scintilla of every moment, each of which constantly changes everything in our future, including the end.

It's crazy, there's the long bit before, then we're born. The best odds anyone appears able to come up with for this to happen, specifically you or me, is 400 trillion to one. Then there's the tiny bit when we're alive, then the long bit after.

So how many people must there be who could have been a genius at something if they'd been given the smallest chance? They just had to be born, have the requisite talent and qualities, in the right place, at the right time, with the right influences and opportunities. All that time, all those places. But what if they weren't that lucky? They were stuck down a coal mine. Died as an infant. Born in a wilderness. Walked round a corner. Were shy. Didn't walk round a corner. They never got near a brush, pen, guitar or even a classroom. The greatest singer-songwriter the world has ever seen never got the chance to write or sing a note.

The Milltown Brothers were fortunate. And would never lay claim to be the greatest or the unluckiest whatever. But what happened to them demonstrates the utterly random nature of life splendidly.

Fast-forward and the idea dropped out of my mind, as most of them do. I'd left the working world where I knew Matthew. We were still in touch, but met only once or twice a year, usually to get drunk and laugh a lot.

Then he called in November 2023 to tell me the Milltown

Brothers were playing a gig. Did I want to come along and make sure there was an audience? The idea for the book jumped out of nowhere into my mind and straight out of my mouth. And he said, *'Why not?'*

I'd come to believe the Milltown Brothers had been – and indeed still were – a bunch of reasonably talented, pleasant, decent, ordinary people. With a glint in their eyes and something else.

One of an admittedly very large group of bands and musicians who could have been much more commercially successful and well known than they were.

More significantly, they were one of a much smaller group of bands who got themselves in a position where they were on the cusp of being exactly that.

All while being ridiculously normal, friendly, flawed and nice with it. Nick Morrell agrees, he's still a mate of theirs. He went to school with them and roadied for them, then spent his entire career in the army and the prison service. In November 2024 he drove the van for them to their sold-out gig at the Lexington in London.

They had the songs, enthusiasm, exposure and backing from a record company. They were blessed with good fortune, plus that something else. The sum of their parts was much greater than a bunch of five individuals who could play and sing a bit. They could do magic. When they got it right, they soared.

Early on they were incredibly lucky, too quickly. They got some big breaks and kept getting them. They had to catch up with themselves under the pitiless eye of the music industry. And possibly never quite did.

From the start it appeared nothing could go wrong. Hope inevitably turned to expectation. Less than four years after the band formed, four brilliantly good things happened in a mad six-month period in 1991, bringing it all to a climax.

Within each there was a twist in the tail. One didn't appear disappointing at all. The next was instantly disappointing and impacted on everything else, but they brushed it off. The other two were slightly slower burners, but their collective impact was quietly devastating. Such that another thing went wrong, and another. Throw in one or two (maybe three or four) terrible decisions, and nothing could stop it all unravelling. Even while they were still enjoying themselves, and apparently on the crest of a wave, in their hearts they knew.

It took three highly entertaining years after things started to go awry, but they snatched obscurity from the jaws of fame. And then they all had to find something else to do.

Such is life, chaotic and utterly random. Fortune favours neither the bold nor the brave nor those who are winning. It's just what happens at every given moment. Those with a different perspective might call it divine intervention, providence or fate, or say that things happen for a reason. It isn't, they don't, it's luck.

And that's why this is no tragedy. It's a celebration, it happened. As Tim Paton, the band's first manager knows: '*Let's face it, very few bands have any career at all. They did stuff they could never have dreamt of.*'

Part 1
BEFORE (1957–1987)

*'Well, it's a story of five friends who do something
unusual and good together.'*
Nian

Cold Meat

Jean Brown was the daughter of a dairy farmer. She married
Edward Nelson in April 1957, and he started working for
G Plan at Clover Mill in Pendle in the early 1960s. Great timing because the company launched their radical Danish range
around the same period, designed by renowned architect Ib
Kofod-Larsen. Not much at all to do with Edward, but there
you go, he was along for the ride. Before retiring in 1989, he
worked his way through the company and ended up managing
director of the upholstery division. All while living 20 minutes
away in the family home in Colne.

Jean and Edward had four children. In order of appearance:
Mark, Simon, Sarah, Matthew. All born in the mill town of
Colne in Lancashire, between 1959 and 1968.

The first performance by any of those who would become
the Milltown Brothers took place in the early summer of 1975
in the garage of the Nelson family home in Colne. Their band
was called Cold Meat. It comprised elder brother Mark Nelson
on lead guitar and vocals, Simon Nelson and neighbour Andy
Marsden on drums, and Sarah and Matthew – the latter just
seven years old – on air guitar.

It was a 12-bar blues jam according to Mark. It's not clear
what it was to Sarah or Matthew. The audience included parents,
neighbours and one cousin.

Sarah, Mark, Matthew and Simon Nelson

Following Joe Cocker's inaugural air guitar performance at Woodstock in 1969 during his cover of the Beatles' 'With a Little Help from My Friends', Cold Meat's may be one of the earliest known recorded occurrences of the phenomenon in the UK – outside of Status Quo fans, obviously. Since 1996 the Air Guitar World Championships have taken place in Oulu in Finland.

Mark Nelson

Mark Nelson was born to Jean and Edward in 1959 in Colne. He's the eldest Nelson brother, but he was never a Milltown Brother. Too old. Too wild. Too daft. Too busy. Although he does occasionally get up on stage with them.

He got the music ball rolling and kept booting it forward.

Mark has always tried hard to have a good time. He's a large, passionate and sensitive soul, a tad intimidating if you don't know him. He says insightful things in a big northern accent. A man of contrast and contradiction. Successful artist and art teacher. Successful rugby union player and coach. A good scrapper and a good man of peace. The most opinionated, outspoken and devil-may-care of the Nelson brothers. And there's one thing

Mark,18, among Angels, USA

the brothers all agree on, including Mark, unsurprisingly. He'd have made the best rock star.

He was the first to board at Lancaster Royal Grammar School for Boys, 50 miles from home. It's not a private school, it's a state school, but unusually it takes boarders. Unlike his brothers to come he loved it, being into art and sport. Sport is particularly good there, but not if you want to play football. They play rugby union and he played on the wing for England Rugby Union schoolboys in 1978.

He studied fine art at Liverpool Polytechnic and teacher training at Carnegie College Leeds. He played, he taught, he coached. He was the backs coach for Sale Sharks when they won the Rugby Union Premiership in 2006. And for all that time he wrote and performed music, wherever and whenever he got the chance, and he still does.

9

In his youth he learned to play both piano and guitar, the latter on a second-hand Burns London Original electric guitar his dad bought him for £10. (He asked me to put that in, said it would amuse and warm some people.) His primary motivation to learn was to impress girls. The first song he could play was 'Something' by the Beatles. He quickly began to write songs. You're unlikely to have heard any of them, but quite a few are out there.

After the Cold Meat gig, he played his next as the Hamptons. It took place in one of the smallest rooms in his school and was *'laid-back and intimate'*. Accompanying him on drums was 12-year-old brother Simon. They had three songs, all covers: 'Bad Moon Rising' by Creedence Clearwater Revival, 'Meet Me on the Corner' by Lindisfarne and 'Arms of Mary' by Sutherland Brothers and Quiver.

The second and final gig played by the Hamptons was in a bigger room at the school in 1977. Brother Simon, now 14, was still on drums. They'd forgotten how to play 'Arms of Mary' but still knew 'Bad Moon Rising' and 'Meet Me on the Corner', and they had *'this bluesy riff, we could play it slow… And we could play it quick.'* They ended up filling the place and had to repeat their just about four-song set. Mark remembers it as a much more rocking gig than the first one, mainly because of the quick version of the bluesy riff and the boisterous crowd. During the third rendition-ing of 'Bad Moon Rising' he realised the audience was beginning to get bored and abruptly ended the show, suggesting they go to the pub. This didn't go down well with the teachers present.

In 1991 Mark played guitar for the exotically named Breezer & Red Squared. (A few years later another of the Milltown Brothers – Barney, not himself a Nelson – appeared in the abridged version of the band, Red Squared.) At Loughborough Students Christmas Ball in 1991, they supported Chesney Hawkes, one of the most famous of one-hit wonders. Although, to be fair, he had one and a half – and 'The One and Only', written by Nik Kershaw, was much bigger than anything the Milltown Brothers did.

After the gig a couple of members of the band got chatting with someone from BMG who happened to be there and was moderately impressed. They came straight to the point. '*I like you but I hate the name and you must get rid of the bouncer on guitar.*'

Mark once played and sang 'Leaving on a Jet Plane' over the PA system to the whole of Manchester Airport. He also played in a band called Big Picture, alongside Barney (again) and Bobby Elliott, a founding member of the '60s British beat combo the Hollies. Big Picture released a cover of Crosby, Stills, Nash & Young's 'Our House' in 2007 as a charity single for Pendleside Hospice. And in 2009 Mark provided both the cover art and co-wrote two songs, including the title track, for the 21st and final Hollies album *Now, Then, Always*.

As for the Milltown Brothers, Mark not only introduced Simon to playing in a band, he also helped him learn to play guitar. And introduced him to the music he liked, which was mostly prog rock. But perhaps his most significant impact on them was to be indirectly responsible for the Milltown Brothers' name. Which may or may not be a good thing.

In the early summer of 1987 Mark played a one-off gig with brother Simon at the Water Witch, a canal side pub in Lancaster. Needing a name for the night, they called themselves the Millionaire Brothers and their eclectic set included covers of the Smiths' 'Heaven Knows I'm Miserable Now', Lindisfarne's indefatigable 'Meet Me on the Corner' and Cockney Rebel's 'Judy Teen', alongside a few of their own songs. Brother Matthew, who was in his first band (The Spire), went along to watch them and jokingly said the Milltown Brothers would have been much better than the Millionaire Brothers. It stuck somewhere in Simon's head.

Mark brought this gig to a close by headbutting a member of the audience as they approached him, having shouted: '*Do you know Bob? Do you know Bob? Do you know Bob?*' ad nauseam for most of the set.

He now lives in Lytham St Annes on the Lancashire coast with his partner, Susan. He's a full-time artist and part-time musician and says the art would make him a reasonable living if he could add a nought or two to what he sold each painting for.

Simon Nelson

Simon Nelson is the elder statesman of the Milltown Brothers. He was born on 2 May 1963. He plays guitar and in partnership with Matthew is the main songwriter for the band. By the time they finally became the Milltown Brothers in December 1987, he was all of 24 years old. He's got at least five years on the rest of them – although an article three years later in the first issue of the short-lived *London Music* magazine suggests someone may occasionally have been liberal with the truth. '*In case you're wondering, Matt, aged 22, and Simon, one year his junior, are the only blood relations in the group.*'

It didn't stop here. Simon is as honest as the day is long, but he did insist in late 1993, in what proved to be the last issue of 'Coming From The Mill', the band's UK fanzine, that he was 27 when he was just about 30. Call it the power of pop – and desperate times – at play. Because of the age gap and the fact that Matthew's friend James was a superb guitarist, he thought he was lucky the others let him in the band. He shouldn't have worried, they loved him.

Nian explains: '*We were lucky to have Simon, we were just young lads… in a school band… and we're making this decision to go to Manchester Poly, we didn't care what we were studying, we just wanted to carry on with the music when our band the Spire was actually a bit shit, not very good, we had nothing to hang on to.*'

And his contribution to the Milltown Brothers would go way beyond the music. Not least because having a pair of genetic brothers reinforced the idea of the brotherly spirit among the band – all deeply true despite industry cynicism. Similar but more inclusive than the Allman Brothers and certainly more authentic than either the Righteous Brothers or the Ramones. Or any of the many iterations of Brotherhood of Man for that matter.

The other members of the band talk about his intelligence, level-headedness, diligence, ability to get stuff done – and persistent attempts to keep them on the relatively straight and narrow. A path he's tried to follow *'with a fair-ish measure of success'* throughout his music career. In the very early days of the Milltown Brothers, he even turned up for most gigs in a suit and tie, straight from work. But always managed to get changed before going on stage.

When he describes himself, we get an alternative picture. Of someone who's essentially pessimistic, who overthinks things and worries, and who is perversely superstitious about the band – and Burnley FC. *'I'd definitely avoid shaving on the day of a gig especially if it was the first day of a tour... never black underpants on gig days... I would always favour left stage in the early days, but we were pushed around as support band so often I had to drop that one. In the recording studio I'd do all I could to avoid looking at the gain gauge on the 24-track recorder and fader on the desk for channel 13 – if the producer put the guitar on channel 13, I would ask to change it... on the way to recording in Bath in May 1992 I was desperately searching for two magpies together but only ever saw one... I knew the session was doomed... I have carried this over into Burnley FC, but it has been proved wrong so many times that it's now defunct.'*

He's terrified of failure too. So he was always loath to pass up any opportunity to promote the band. Even if the vehicle was – frankly – inappropriate. Ergo playing live on *Blue Peter*, *Wogan* and even *Going Live!* – on which, far too early in the morning of Saturday 16 February 1991 and after having played a crazy gig in Wolverhampton the night before, the band played 'Which Way Should I Jump?' live from BBC Television Centre, White City. (A ridiculously enthusiastic and bouncy young compère called Phillip Schofield introduced and interviewed the band.)

Simon was the second Nelson brother to attend and board at Lancaster Grammar. He was keen to disassociate himself from the drums and used a Yamaha acoustic and Telecaster copy to learn to play guitar, both owned by Mark.

'I guess first learning to play in early 1980, I was very influenced by all the punk and new wave bands I'd listened to. Initially I thought of it as a vehicle for songwriting and showing off, so the downstroke chug and crash chord styles of the likes of the Undertones, the Jam, the Cars, the Pistols etc. seemed to make sense, although obviously I learned later there was miles more sophistication in the likes of John and Damian O'Neill's playing. As I got more confident, I was certainly influenced by the magnificent jangle and angular playing of people like James Honeyman-Scott, Johnny Marr, Frank Infante, Chris Stein, Tom Verlaine and, most important of all, Peter Buck.'

He wanted to disassociate himself from the school too, despite his intelligence. He particularly didn't like having to board there and hated being called a *'fucking grammar stiff'* in the street. He wrote many tearful letters home.

He wasn't even in the cool set of boys in his year, or their band. So he formed his own, The Spies, with Patrick, the geography teacher's son, on piano. He sang, played guitar and wrote songs. They played at school Film Society nights and entered an Ormskirk young songwriters' competition. They didn't win. Their career highlight was headlining a street party on 29 July 1981 in Lancaster – celebrating the wedding of Prince Charles and Lady Diana Spencer.

All would agree Simon is the most academic of the Nelson brothers. He did well at school and went to Nottingham University, emerging in 1986 with a decent degree in French. While he was there he met Rachel, who a few years later would become his wife and happily still is.

In his first year he formed a band with Ian Mellanby on bass and Ian Bell on drums. They weren't much good. And they weren't much good with names. They looked at the racing page in a discarded *Daily Mirror* for guidance and somehow a horse called Tropical Blue jumped out at them. They decided to ride it.

Tropical Blue's first gig? Supporting the Polecats – rockabilly stalwarts – at Nottingham University. In June 1984 they stepped a little further out of the shadows, entering a Battle of the Bands competition at the legendary Rock City in Nottingham, hosted by Radio 1 DJ Janice Long. First prize was a Radio 1 session. You got nothing for coming second – and they came second. But Janice took a fancy to them and offered a Radio 1 session anyway. Euphoria, they were on their way.

Simon picks up the story. *'A few weeks later we'd still heard nothing about the session and a creeping concern was sinking in. The Radio 1 Roadshow was on a large barge, winding its merry way along the Leeds Liverpool canal – with Janice aboard. It was due to pass through Blackburn and I convinced myself if I could get to it and grab Janice's attention in person she'd sort it. It was the summer and I was home from Nottingham, so I got my dad to drive me to the right spot. As the barge approached I saw Janice and shouted, "Janice, it's Simon from Tropical Blue… the Rock City Battle of the Bands thing… radio session…" Janice smiled, seemed to recognise me and shouted back, asking if I'd like to join them on the barge for the day, enjoy the party. I still cringe and blush when I recall the 12 words that came out of my mouth in response: "I'm sorry, I can't. My dad's waiting for me in the car."'*

The session did eventually happen but didn't go well. It was quietly broadcast on Radio 1 on Ian Brass's show at 7.30 in the evening on Saturday, 15 December 1984. Three years later Simon and Matthew wrote what they call their first proper songs, among them 'Janice Is Gone', which the Milltown Brothers recorded at Strawberry Studios in Stockport in 1988.

The disappointment of the session and the move to Paris didn't deter Tropical Blue. Both Ians decamped and lived on Simon's floor until the summer of 1985. In early 1985 they decided Tropical Blue wasn't a great name and changed it. Good move.

The Word Association

Simon Nelson: Vocals / Guitar / Songwriter
Ian Mellanby: Bass
Ian Bell: Drums, until July 1985
Jean-Brice Vietri: Drums, from July 1985

Simon, second right

The Word Association managed a handful of gigs in Paris, including at the veteran rock club Gibus. It's still open today, one of the leading gay clubs in the French capital.

At the end of the summer term via a friend who worked for NAT Holidays, the band got themselves a lovely job playing a circuit of campsites and bars in the south of France for the summer. Off they went. The Ian's fell out and drummer Ian disappeared into the night with his French girlfriend. Desperately in need of a drummer, the band were introduced to a local, Jean-Brice Vietri. Jean ended up staying with the band until, two years or so later, they called it a day – in Nottingham and London as well as Marseillan Plage and Cap d'Agde.

It would be putting it mildly to say the band enjoyed what turned out to be three summers playing the circuit in the south of France, living in tents until the last summer when they borrowed a small apartment from one of Jean-Brice's dad's friends. Each year they played 40 or 50 gigs from mid-June to September. A mix of covers – from the likes of the Beatles, Elvis Costello, the Undertones and U2 – and Simon's originals.

On returning to the UK, the Word Association released their one and only independent single in October 1985: the harmonica-driven 'Mary Mary' backed with 'The Ballad of Tina Rose' on Crocker Records, both written by Simon. 'Mary, Mary' features on *C85*, a 3CD release from Cherry Red records offering *'the best of the burgeoning indie scene.'* Along with small headline gigs the band's support slots into 1986 included Mighty Mighty, Richard Jobson's Armoury Show and the June Brides. All of this proper band stuff was being admired and envied from afar by Matthew and his school friends James and Nian.

Unbeknown to them, though, Simon wasn't feeling much like a musician. After finishing university and their second summer season in the south of France in 1986 the band decided to move to a grim Finchley bedsit in London, to give the music a go.

In contrast to the south of France in summer, *'a shithole'* in Finchley in winter lacks a certain charm. They were on the dole, they were freezing, they were damp. Their dole cheques kept getting stolen by tramps. Tramps who frequently dossed in the bathroom. But they did manage a couple of demo sessions and sent out an 8-track demo tape. It achieved nothing.

Simon remembers it as an increasingly desperate time. The dark, cold months were interminable. Nothing much ever seemed to happen. But they did play a handful of gigs in London and Lancaster. Twice at the Timebox Club in the Bull & Gate – a pub (almost) next door to the Town & Country Club in Kentish Town – in 1986 and 1987. Little more than a year later he'd be back at the Bull & Gate with the Milltown Brothers, a pivotal gig in their career… and within another year of that the Milltown Brothers would play at the Town & Country Club itself.

In February 1987, the Word Association played a gig at the Brown Cow in Lancaster, supported by the Spire, the band brother Matthew had formed with his school friends James and Nian. Two months later the lease on the flat was up and the Word Association had all had enough of Finchley. Another summer in the south of France lay ahead, but Finchley had been a harsh dose of reality.

Simon moved back to the family home, caught a gig by the Spire at the Park Hotel in Lancaster and began working for a few weeks at Colne library, before heading off to the south of France – with brother Matthew in tow – to play that final summer with The Word Association. The band played their last gig together in Cap d'Agde in early September 1987.

But Simon wasn't done with music. On the contrary, working in Colne Library wasn't the only thing he'd been doing before the final south of France trip.

Matthew Nelson

Matthew Nelson was born on 20 March 1968 in Colne. He's the singer (he even wrote a song to prove it, called 'I'm a Singer'), main songwriter and the creative heartbeat (say the other members of the band, not him) of the Milltown Brothers. Given what he was doing – and how he was doing it – when I met him in 2004, I find this difficult to get my head around. The point when you meet people and the assumptions you inevitably form is frighteningly arbitrary, demonstrating how we can have only one view of the world, when there is an infinity at any given moment and an infinity of moments.

Matthew is admirably indifferent to his past and, as you already know, rarely talks about himself. Out of the spotlight he's always been quiet, and in the background, he can appear unemotional, withdrawn and uninterested. But when persuaded – say when you're writing a book that involves him – he'll tell you he's a songwriter and his singing voice is something he honed out of limited resources to express his songs. Songwriting is what he discovered he could do and what makes it worthwhile. Happily he wrote and demoed a song called 'So You Want to be a Writer' – as well as 'I'm a Singer'. It eventually appeared on *More Slinky*, a compilation album released only in Japan in the autumn of 1991.

The other thing you need to know about Matthew is that he openly admits to being bottom of the class academically. School didn't work for him. This is hard to figure given his songwriting ability and the spontaneity and dynamism he brings to his role as lead singer and ringmaster on stage. He has a nerveless, passionate and mildly possessed persona, and tells me he's always felt very comfortable on stage. It was his safe place, surrounded by his mates. Gave him the sense of being set free. Although he admits his stage banter never amounted to very much: *'This is our favourite song...'* on repeat, after many, many different songs.

Plus the occasional misjudged rant, all of which is at odds with the songs he writes. These have most often been described as poetic. Typically heartfelt stories and allegories about love, loss, joy, yearning, belonging and... self-doubt. The best are streams of consciousness, just what pours out of him. Fans love the everyday life passions they articulate, critics think they can be over-sentimental and romantic, with insufficient questioning of the world and its injustices. More soft Kerouac than hard Dylan. And he's never been comfortable talking about them. *'Whenever I explain a song it dies on me, they are metaphors for losing your innocence,'* he told *Vox*, August 1991.

This more recent reflection is a more honest and helpful interpretation, and would have stood him in good stead in 1991. *'I just write whatever comes out of my head when we've got a melody or riff and other people can decide what it's about for them when it's left me. The easier the words come and instinctively knowing where they are going to go, the better the song. Where the words go is a pretty loose exercise, yet it makes or breaks everything. As for the meaning, there's no considered thought behind it; it really is a stream of consciousness when it works best and whatever the words are, they're as close to a raw expression of me, my essence, who I am as anything could be. I don't understand what's wrong with that. They're the outpourings of a normal person with a head and a heart who wasn't great at school, it's what I want to get across. Let's face it, most singers who think they have something important to say didn't start life as a philosopher or whatever. It's easy to fall flat on your face if it's a facade and you're singing about stuff that you maybe think will make the music be taken more seriously by the world. I'm not saying protest singers aren't genuine in their beliefs – you know how the band feel about Dylan – but I want it to be instinctive and don't want to force myself to think too much about it and try writing about stuff I know nothing about. It's like lying and could mess with the tune.'*

It's no surprise to learn that as a young boy he loved his own company, his first childhood memories dominated by time he spent alone. At junior school he found things hard going. His dad performed a minor miracle or two to get him through the eleven-plus. Matthew has no idea how he managed to pass and can't remember a thing about it.

One of the few things to bring him out of himself was his love of Burnley Football Club. A fondness shared by Simon and the rest of the Milltown Brothers – more or less; don't believe everything you read in the press. James was never a football fan but was happy to go along with it. Nian comes from a family of ardent Liverpool supporters and was certainly never a member of Burnley's youth football team, despite being an excellent player, but given Liverpool's self-evident superiority he was happy for Burnley to be his second club for PR purposes.

Matthew's most vivid early memories of attending football matches relate more to what happened just about off the pitch than on it. He vividly remembers a midweek game against Celtic in the – not sadly missed – Anglo-Scottish Cup when he was 10. Turf Moor – Burnley's ground – became a battlefield. Rival fans ripped up railings and terracing and used them as spears and clubs. Separated from his mate and his mate's dad, he was escorted to a quieter spot by a policeman and told not to move if he valued his life. It happened again the following Saturday against Sunderland.

Football was his weekends. And so, unsurprisingly, was this: he became the third Nelson brother to board at Lancaster Grammar and he hated it.

But funnily, his educational struggles got better while apparently becoming much worse. He performed so poorly in his second year that the school suggested he stay down and do the year again. Which turned out to be lucky because waiting for

Nian 2nd right, James right

him in the class in that year below were James, Nian, Nick and Max. Two of them would eventually become Milltown Brothers, while the other two would do anything and everything to help the band do their thing. All in one class – and one of four classes he could have been put in. Very lucky. And through a mangle of sport, music and a shared sense of humour, plus Matthew hating the dumb bullying and middle-class laddish mentality dominating the boarders' lives, he gradually found his natural place among them.

Come the early summer of 1985, James and Nian did what they'd kept saying they were going to do and formed a 'post-punk metal' band, Warning. The two of them got into the habit of going to Nian's house during the holidays, then lunch breaks and weekends in term time (he lived close to the school) to watch videos of music programmes and do a bit of very basic music themselves. When he could during term Matthew joined them and occasionally helped them help themselves to some of Nian's dad's home brew.

Decent music programmes were few and far between. Nian recorded bits of *Top of the Pops*, *The Old Grey Whistle Test* and the odd live show that turned up somewhere on BBC 2 or the relatively fresh-faced Channel 4. But the show they loved was *The Tube*. It appeared on Channel 4 for the first time on Bonfire Night in 1982. A brilliant, irreverent alternative to *Top of the Pops*, giving exposure to many alternative, post-punk and indie bands and musicians. And with a much cooler, more discerning youth audience. It became a polarising influence for Matthew, James and Nian, encouraging the convergence of their musical interests. REM made their first appearance outside the *USA* on The Tube on 18 November 1983 – the day before playing their first UK gig at Dingwalls in Camden.

The next time REM were on *The Tube* was October 1985. By then Matthew had briefly visited Simon as the Word Association played their first tour in the south of France earlier that summer and had his first experience of being on stage. This proved somewhat challenging, an experience best left to everyone's imagination. REM played the sublime 'Driver 8' on *The Tube* that night, four days after Matthew and Simon had seen them play it and 23 other songs at Rock City in Nottingham. Two nights later they saw Prefab Sprout play there too, in support of their second album *Steve McQueen*.

Between these REM TV appearances, and in addition to his visit to the south of France, Matthew had begun to teach himself guitar sufficiently well to use it to write what he calls *'sort of…'* songs. And *'doing bits and pieces of music and stuff'* while hanging out with James and Nian. Motivated by what they and Simon were up to, he decided that being a singer/songwriter was something he might be able to do. A career choice. He just had to find the songs, the voice and the band. After the REM and Prefab Sprout gigs in Nottingham his mind was made up. *'I didn't have any other career in my head by the time I was 17 or so. Luckily I was friends with a great guitar player and a drummer. I think I became happy to be a singer when I was in the south of France the first time, other than I couldn't really sing and my songs were awful, but you know. Warning had played a couple of gigs in Lancaster, but Nian didn't like metal, he was mad about Echo & the Bunnymen, and James was up for anything. Conveniently the summer break and a load of new influences put paid to Warning.'*

Autumn term 1985. Writing a bit. Playing a bit. Singing a bit. Watching plenty. Matthew and James trying to work out a few songs, admiring Simon and the Word Association – and their 'Mary Mary' single release – from afar. Come the new year, with James on guitar and Nian on drums, they formed the Spire in February 1986, recruiting classmate Craig Holden on bass.

Six months later, at the beginning of the final school year in September 1986, Matthew, James and Nian had this crazy idea to go to Manchester Poly together and see if they could make the music work. Sensibly Craig decided quietly to leave them to it at the end of school life in 1987. What Matthew chose to study at Manchester was irrelevant, other than making sure he got there. He decided Hotel and Catering Management was within his power. Two Es were required. He managed two Es.

James Fraser

James Fraser was born in Sale, Lancashire on 1 November 1968. All Saints' Day. His family moved to Scale Hall on the outskirts of Lancaster when he was two. His dad was a civil engineer at the nuclear power station on the Lancashire coast at Heysham.

Early life was comfortable enough but tense and difficult at times as a result of three things. Firstly, despite the nature of his job, his dad seemed to be in and out of work and money was often scarce. Secondly his younger sister Holly was unwell and in and out of hospital as a child. And, to top it all, he went to a Catholic primary school.

Even though he was never bullied, he never thought he belonged, finding the other children wild, noisy and hard to get on with. As to the ritualisation and enforcement of religion in school, it was a nightmare and violently put him off organised Western religion. Priests were regular visitors, corporal punishment the norm. Like all the boys he received the sacraments and went to confession. But while the others seemed to balance it effortlessly with a rough and mischievous side, he couldn't and feels if he'd stayed at the school he'd have struggled. Fortunately he told his mum and she got him out of it and into a village-based state school where his sisters went. It was a breath of fresh air and he passed his eleven-plus easily. Next stop Lancaster Royal Grammar School. Not as a boarder, he was local.

It's pretty obvious that discovering the guitar helped him get through the primary school experience. His mum and dad got him a cheap acoustic for Christmas when he was about 9. And while being eternally grateful, James animatedly – for him – insists *'it was as much like a real guitar as a Lego car is a real car.'* (Accurate descriptions are important to him in regard to everything musical.) He started playing, though, and got obsessed. Rushing home every night from primary school to just play and get lost in it.

He can't read music and learned to play by ear, listening over and over to cassette tapes and finding his own way – as Barney did when he discovered the piano. He developed a passion for heavy rock and metal and eventually got himself an electric guitar.

His guitar teacher was more than happy to take him down the Thin Lizzy, Black Sabbath and Saxon route to playing. He's arguably the most accomplished and committed musician among the Milltown Brothers, Barney being the other candidate. Nian knew. *'James was good from day one with Warning, then the Spire and then the Milltown Brothers. He could play and we were novices. He'd pick up a riff and it would instantly sound like a song, it made us, carried us, we seemed far better than we were.'*

What I like about James is that en route to his mid-50s he has acquired and retained at least five different names – and is more than happy to be called any of them. It suggests he doesn't take himself too seriously, despite an earnest and studied disposition. So many people think their name is ridiculously important. It's just an appendage your parents give you, it has nothing innately to do with you.

He's James. Jim. Fraz. Dogman. Hairy Dogman. They get looser and looser. He was christened Dogman – or Hairy Dogman if you prefer the unabridged version – by Matthew in 1983, after noticing his hairy legs during swimming at school and being hairless in that department himself.

Not sure who the joke's on here.

He's the most measured, softly spoken and considered of the band – but with a certain self-possession and engaging sense of humour that made him popular at Lancaster Grammar, which belies his diffidence and natural social awkwardness. Often lost for words, he thinks he can appear, at best, subdued and boring. He talks carefully about his ability – or inability – to process things. It's extraordinary he's appeared on stage in front of all those people. Hundreds of times. And always, on the face of it, happy and confident to do so, I suggest. *'I'm too wrapped up in what I'm doing to notice. I know exactly what I have to do and after the gig a few drinks and a smoke or two does the trick.'*

His first band 'experience' was with Nick, who couldn't and can't play anything. Bigpigs. They worked out song lyrics between them during English classes, dealing with such fertile topics as the horrors of the abattoir, from a pig's perspective.

Much more compelling than Keats' 'Ode to a Nightingale'. Then James took the lyrics home, strummed a tune around them and played and sung them back to Nick. That was it.

At the same time Nian was going around to James' house to accompany his guitar playing, using a pair of chopsticks, chair arm and a couple of cushions. Eventually he got a second-hand drum kit for Christmas in 1984... and by the start of summer term 1985 Warning existed. Nian at the back, Tom Myall and James on vocals and guitars and Matthew Chalmers on bass.

Tom and Matthew lived in Caton, a few miles outside of Lancaster. They rehearsed in the garage of Matthew's mum and dad. It was hard work when there were no parents to give James and Nian a lift with their gear: they had to get the bus and take a mile hike up a steep hill, with electric guitar, amp and full drum kit in a couple of bin bags. And then take it all the way back to catch the bus home. At least that bit was downhill.

Their admirable persistence paid off. They got some songs together and played a few gigs. The first of these was in the summer at Beaumont College, which was for children and young adults with multiple learning difficulties, run by what would become Scope, then known as the National Spastics Society. It wouldn't be the last time Beaumont College loomed large in James' life.

Their second gig was in 1985 at a Keep Music Live event at Lancaster's Sugarhouse – in subsequent years they'd play there as part of both the Spire and the Milltown Brothers. Weirdly given his abject memory about much of the past – if not unsurprising given his musical focus – James remembers unprompted the opening of the Sugarhouse performance. *'It was an utter nightmare... my guitar was out of tune from the very first chord.'*

What happened next? The summer holidays and those influences – REM, the Waterboys, Echo & the Bunnymen – and the indie-driven the Spire slowly rising from the ashes of Warning. James is completely unable to remember anything about the Brown Cow gig when the Spire supported the Word Association in February 1987. But he can remember getting to know Matthew's brother Simon a lot better, just before his final school exams in April and at about the same time he was offered a place to do Business Studies at Manchester Poly, an offer that delighted him but thoroughly disappointed his teachers. They knew him to be capable of much more. Apparent apathy set against potential. They expected him to at least be going to a 'proper' university to study an academic subject. James couldn't care less; all he wanted to do was music.

Nian Brindle

Nian Dylan Brindle was born in Lancaster on 12 February 1969. His dad was a driver, his mum a schoolteacher. He has a brother Seth, five years younger, who remains his best friend outside the band. Seth and his children were at the sold-out Milltown Brothers at the Lexington on Pentonville Road, the one Nick drove the van to, in November 2024.

His parents were still in their teens when they had Nian. Very much cool people of their time, much younger in both age and outlook than most of his friends' parents. Huge Dylan fans if you hadn't noticed. And life was pretty communal for downtown Lancaster. *There were people hanging about the house at all times*

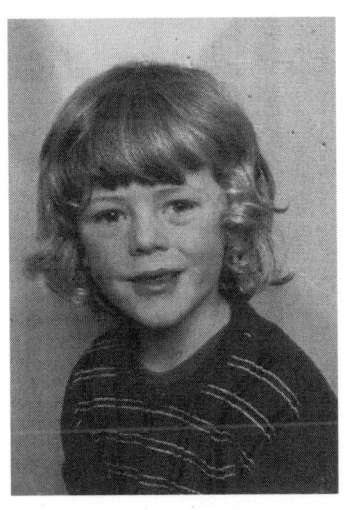

of the day and night, doing this, doing that, drinking, sleeping, smoking, sleeping, tai chi, staring into space, whatever.'

A rugby-playing hippy, his dad still got into punk in the late 70s – loved the anarchic lyrics – and had a copy of 'God Save The Queen' by the Sex Pistols. Nian was 9 and *'borrowed'* it to play at the home of his best mate at primary school, Ian 'Scotty' Moorhouse. Many years later Scotty, who would learn to play the didgeridoo of all things, would go on to form a band, Greenheart, with James. The national press furore regarding punk meant Scotty's grandma, who was looking after him, refused to let Nian play it and sent him home. He blushes about it to this day.

Home was a small-terraced house in a bunch of narrow streets butting up to the playing fields of Lancaster Grammar. Nice juxtaposition. His dad regarded work simply as a means to an end, the end being sport and music. Nian's not much different. There wasn't any money in the house, but they had a superb stereo system to complement their vast record collection. And his dad had been an outstanding rugby union player for the Vale of Lune, where Nelson brothers Mark and Simon, then Nian would also play. In the mid-1970s when union was still an amateur sport, his dad was offered a professional contract by Halifax rugby league, but didn't fancy it.

His mum kept the family on the rails while his dad had a tendency to occasionally drift off them.

He happily regaled the rather conservative members of Vale of Lune rugby club – pillar of the
local community with many ties to Lancaster Grammar School – with his transcendental hippy experiences. Meanwhile Mum was persuading Nian – a good footballer – to go to school there. But they played rugby, not football, and so even though he'd passed his eleven-plus and had been offered a place, he was reluctant to go. His mum solved the problem by finding Nian a local Sunday League team – Marsh United. And then he became a good rugby player at school too.

Nian knew Max first – at primary school – and then Nick,

before any of the others crossed paths, except for the Nelson brothers of course. Nick didn't go to the same primary school, but they were both good footballers and played in the same Lancaster Schools team where Nian was the captain.

Being sports mad and more than handy at any sport he tried was brilliant for him at Lancaster. Like James' sense of humour, it made Nian popular and feel he belonged. And he thinks that musically percussion is ideal for sporty people. Being all about good hand–eye coordination, making an effort, hitting something frequently as hard as you can... and delivering a noise bang on time. He really did start out with chopsticks and the chair arm and James on guitar and was desperate for some proper ones to hit, which is why he ended up going with his mum to pick up a second-hand kit from the vicarage in the village of Cockerham for Christmas in 1984.

Atypically for a drummer, Nian is outgoing and articulate. He's the other Milltown Brother I knew when I first popped Matthew the question about this book; he'd often helped out when Matthew and I were making adverts and stuff. Given the Milltown Brothers' distinct lack of anyone who could speak effectively with the press – and his leadership skills demonstrated on the sports field – I end up wondering whether they could have pushed him more to the fore, unusual for a drummer I accept. When I suggest this to the rest of the band, hilarity follows. They point me to YouTube and that performance of 'Which Way Should I Jump?' on *Going Live!* and the strained interview with Phillip Schofield afterwards. The band look like choir boys (minus the cassocks and surplices), albeit obviously hungover and not saying much at all. James and Nian skulk at the back while Matthew mumbles something about *'no money to buy clothes'* and *'we're ragamuffins'* before tailing off into silence. Nian jumps in and has a go at stringing a coherent sentence or two together about their influences and style... then starts to repeat himself with a couple of flailing open armed gestures. It doesn't look that bad to me, particularly as the question was daft and no one else was saying anything.

He's also empathetic, he gets people, while not wasting his words. *'School was terrible for boarders, they didn't have their own life, but they kept themselves apart. Matthew was different. It's never been on his radar to think he was better than anyone else just because his mum and dad could afford for him to board at school. And he carried none of that impregnable air of confidence unlike the rest of them. I found him easy to talk to and after I'd nervously asked him round to my house a couple of times, I told him how crap I felt about where I lived compared to everyone else. He just told me I had a lovely family home, he really loved coming over – and that he'd like to be able to go home every night. I realised then everyone has their hang-ups and insecurities.'*

As to the music, he got into Echo & the Bunnymen and saw them at Lancaster University in October 1984 on the Ocean Rain tour. It was a huge thing for him and it all mushroomed with Matthew and James. Then he discovered girls. Then he got involved with Warning, followed by the Spire. Then he got a long-term girlfriend, Suzanne, who was Nian's first love; they were inseparable until 1992. Then he read *On the Road* by Jack Kerouac and realised life might be *'just for kicks'*, and certainly much bigger than Lancaster. Then his education was sacrificed because of all these other *then*s... In his A levels he managed just two Ds and an E.

Which is why he ended up being the last one, ages after Matthew and James, to get a place at Manchester Poly, scrambling through clearing and getting to do Geography and European Studies. Which is also why he ended up in a student house in Stretford, on the other side of Manchester from James and Matthew in Didsbury.

The Spire

Matthew Nelson: Vocals / Songwriter
James Fraser: Guitar / Songwriter
Nian Brindle: Drums
Craig Holden: Bass

James, Nian, Matthew and Craig

So, the name…? The band could see the spire of Lancaster Cathedral from the room in the school where they rehearsed.

In February 1986 they started making a noise whenever they got the chance to play together, into a ghetto blaster with a built-in microphone, and Matthew shouting his head off in order to be heard. The first of a number of Nelson/Fraser compositions they demoed in this way was a song called 'Crown of Thorns'. The quality was terrible and only one tape was made of every song. So other than when they played it back together, they ended up passing it round in slow circulation to chew over.

Within a couple of months they organised and paid for their first recording session at the Lancaster Musicians Co-op – a huge moment. Mick Armistead engineered the session and held their hands. Mick would later play keyboards on James' third album, *One Man Clapping*, recorded live over two nights at Moles, the club in Bath, a place that would later become extremely familiar to the Milltown Brothers.

Says Nian: *'The first time we ever went into a studio down at the musicians Co-op just round the corner from where I lived…*

Mick Armistead, who's a lovely bloke, set everything up for us. We just stood around in a bit of a daze, didn't have a clue what we were doing. Then we got round to playing something and the first time we went upstairs to hear what we'd done it was just like "Oh my god" – you know, hearing the bass drum, then the snare come through the studio desk and it sounds like something I'd heard on record before, it actually sounded quite good and I'm like, Is that me?'

They demoed three songs, 'City of the Dreaming Spires', 'Progress' and 'Salford Lady'. The last-named grabbed elder brother Simon's attention when he heard it: it's one of the darkest and most aggressive songs Matthew has written, about Myra Hindley and her attempts to be released from jail around that time. Driven by James' guitar, it jangles along in something approximating to what would become Milltown Brothers fashion. But Matthew's vocal is a one-off, deep, forceful and emotionally charged, predating similarly committed grunge vocals by a couple of years. The song resurfaced seven years later as an easier-going Milltown Brothers song, 'Sweet Nothing', the B-side for the vinyl single of Dylan cover 'It's All Over Now, Baby Blue'.

During May half-term, the Spire played their first gig. At the Gregson Centre, only a few minutes' walk from school. As with their first session, the band made all the arrangements, booking and paying for it themselves. Convinced they were ready one minute but thoroughly unconvinced the next. By turn loving the thrill, then shellshocked and terrified at what they'd done.

A week before they were due to play, they'd sold all the tickets. And written and practised 12 original songs plus a couple of covers for the night. Among them 'Salford Lady', 'I've Got a Cousin Who Lives Upstairs' – *'He identifies himself by the clothes he wears, He used to be a Bolshevik but now he's insane…'.* Matthew admits: *'Yes… In large parts it was all very sixth form.'*

They played two sets of seven songs each. Matthew thinks it must have been boring, but both the band and partisan crowd loved it. Elder brother Mark was there, standing out like a sore thumb. He loved it too. Nian's diary tells us the band managed a two-song encore. And he managed six pints.

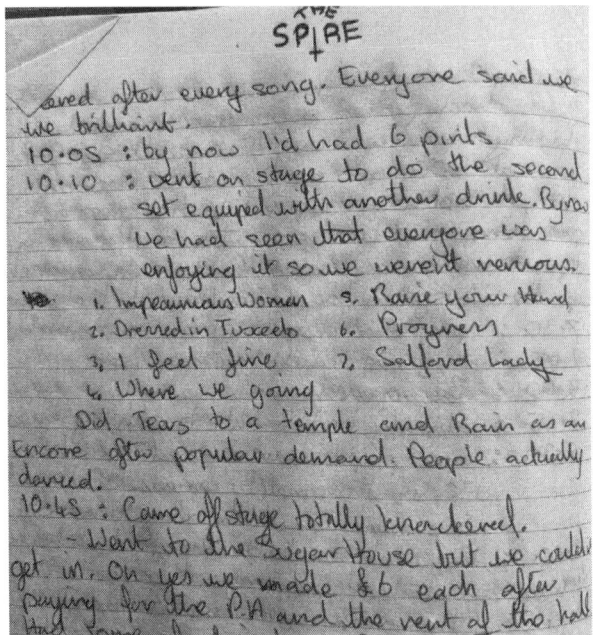

Nian's diarised first gig night

They went on to play a handful of gigs in and around Lancaster during 1986 and early 1987. Including at the Water Witch, where the Millionaire Brothers – Mark and Simon – later played and Matthew uttered the words *'Milltown Brothers'* for the first time.

They were determined to take every opportunity, whatever got in their way. At St Martin's College – a venue also played by Simon and the Word Association – James played sat in a chair with his leg in a plaster cast as a result of a fall from his bike.

At the Red Well Country Inn in Arkholme, 10 miles from Lancaster, they struggled to get their gear over in a borrowed car and set up in front of a handful of disinterested regulars. The first song they played was a cover of a Police song, 'De Doo Doo Doo, De Da Da Da'. As they ended their opener the landlord of the pub walked over to Matthew, whispered in his ear and walked off. The rest of the band were eager to know what he'd said. *'You're shit, pack up and fuck off.'*

They decided they were going nowhere – it had been a nightmare getting there – so they brazened it out to the bitter end with their entire set. Before doing as the landlord suggested.

Enthused, they had their second session at the Lancaster Musicians Co-op, demoing 'I've Got a Cousin ...', 'Heavenly Majesty', 'Secondhand News', 'Fisherman' and 'Girls Don't Cry'.

The decision to go to higher education together to do the band thing may have been a flight of fancy, but once it was made, going to Manchester Poly was a no-brainer. The city was coming alive musically, they were all pretty sure of getting in and it was close enough to all their homes to move stuff back and forth... and get Nick and Max's help and support.

The Spire did their third and final session at the Lancaster Musicians Co-op around the time of their gig with the Word

Handmade A4 gig posters

Association at the Brown Cow. 'My Country', 'One in a Million' and 'Hey There Little Girl' were the resulting demos.

After the Brown Cow gig and with final exams looming, they played what proved to be their last gig at the Park Hotel in Lancaster in April 1987, with brother Simon in the audience.

Barnaby 'Barney' Williams

Barnaby James Williams is the baby of the band, born in Burnley on 5 June 1969. Not only is he the youngest, he was also, by some distance, the last piece of the Milltown Brothers to arrive. They met him at Manchester Poly, even though he was brought up round the corner from the Nelsons in Burnley.

Always known as Barney, he's part of a close-knit family, from Padiham on the western edge of Burnley. They lived with his paternal grandfather, while next door his mum's sister lived with her family and Barney's maternal grandparents.

Barney with football and family friends

His dad, William Williams, was a jobbing solicitor in town in his father-in-law's small local practice. And a chain-smoker – Barney remembers going to sit with him in his grotty office at the weekends strewn with box files and papers, the air thick with cigarette smoke. In 1997 he died aged 68 from leukaemia.

Barney was very close to his mum, Gaye, a volunteer Justice of the Peace. He describes her as a wonderful woman and is clearly moved when he talks about her death in 2013. He attributes his outlook on life to a positive take on her pet phrase about the family: *'What we do is make the best of a bad lot.'* And he's adamant their's wasn't a bad lot.

His best childhood friend was the family St Bernard, Brandy, who went everywhere with him. And he is still close to his brother, Mark, and sister, Helen. The family had a piano that his dad liked to knock out a tune on. When Helen started taking lessons, so did Barney aged 8, but he didn't enjoy the classical approach of his teacher Mr Sutcliffe and gave it up after a couple of months.

Despite this, he would eventually find a way to become the keyboard player in the Milltown Brothers, and team up with Mr Sutcliffe again at a slightly later date. For quite a while in the band, he preferred to be known as Barney James. One of his great heroes, Ray Charles, used his middle name as his last name for career purposes. Barney thought that was cool but eventually just forgot and reverted to his last name.

He challenges James for being the driest wit in the band and, indeed, most obsessive musician – while being much more manic with it. In many ways he looks as innocuous and cute as a mouse – but he has a kick like a mule. He talks in a deep northern accent, vibrantly alive, a pithy person who gets on with life extremely quickly, in all manner of ways. The tiny bits as much as the big bits.

James knows him best off all: *'Barney is a bit bonkers. He's spent his whole life just being busy, he can never sit still, he's always got somewhere to go, but he's a great lad, I love him and we shared a room together when we were away. We're like chalk and cheese but*

*get on brilliantly, same sense of humour, he brings me out of myself
and gets me going.'*

He's probably the biggest Burnley FC fan of all among the
band. Matthew disagrees vehemently, despite Barney being a
season ticket holder from the age of 6. When he was 16 or so,
he used to pile into the back of a Transit van with 20 others to
get to away games. He was friends with most of the hardcore
Burnley football hooligans who became known affectionately as
the Suicide Squad in the 1980s. Fighting at football wasn't his
thing, but inside a boxing ring it was a different matter and from
the age of 10 he was part of the Old Mill boxing club. He loved
the fitness and discipline and had a handful of amateur bouts
before his mum blamed his increasingly bad migraines on the
boxing and begged him to stop. Which he did, but he was never
going to have a humdrum adolescence.

*'I was 16 and me and my friend Nick were stranded after a
party with no taxi money. We walked to the nearest village and
found an Escort RS 1600 with the keys in it, so we jumped in. I
drove because I had been driving bangers on my mate's farm for a
while. The idea was to drop Nick off and leave the car somewhere
near my house, but we had a blowout on the country roads, so we
scouted around and found a Capri with keys in too and tried to
continue the mission, but unfortunately I crashed it into a wall. I
wasn't particularly proud of myself and certainly wasn't going to do
it again. Time passed and we thought we'd got away with it, but
another lad we vaguely knew had been nicking cars and six months
later he got arrested. They were trying to pin these two on him, so
he grassed us up and we got arrested. As my dad was a local solicitor
and Nick's dad a sergeant in the police, we made the front page of
the* Burnley Express. *I had to sell my motorbike to pay the fine and
got banned from driving (I was 17 by the time we got done) for 12
months.'*

Barney hadn't enjoyed his time at Queen Elizabeth Grammar
School, Blackburn, his destination after passing the eleven-plus.
First chance he got to leave, he went to Nelson & Colne College.
He was no star pupil but discovered a love for acting while he was

there, having initially been press-ganged into it. He applied for a place at RADA, but decided not to pursue his interview when they asked him to bring along his leotard. The idea of him having to have a leotard was enough.

Not much of a fan of early 1980s music, he'd begun listening to his dad's vinyl collection and discovered Oscar Peterson, Ray Charles and Aretha Franklin among others. His brother had also introduced him to ska and two-tone. One lunchtime in his first year at college, he found himself in the music department and heard a guy called Adrian Douthwaite tinkering 12-bar blues melodies on the piano. Mesmerised, he asked him what and how he was playing.

At home that evening, he couldn't wait to get to the family piano. It had been sat for years doing not very much. He jumped on it, started teaching himself and carried on – day-in, day-out. He had a ghetto blaster with cassette tapes and listened repeatedly to the tiniest snippets of Ray Charles and Oscar Peterson that grabbed him. And found his way to reproduce them on the piano. Jazz, blues and boogie-woogie piano were his thing.

It wasn't long before Barney's ability to improve on the piano had plateaued. He needed to find someone who could take him to the next level, and did so in the shape of Patricia Schofield. She taught jazz piano from her home in Blackburn, having majored in jazz on the piano at Leeds College of Music. He loved it and was determined to pursue a career in music, but with no qualifications at all in music or piano, music college was a non-starter.

Unaware of the existence of Simon, or Matthew, Nian and James and their plan to go to Manchester Poly in the autumn of 1987, he decided on his own to do more or less the same thing. Manchester looked like a good place to get involved with music in a more grass roots, social kind of way, it had a strong jazz tradition and was handy for home too. He got offered a place on an HND Business Studies course, at just about the same time as he got involved with his first band in Burnley.

Plastic Spearmen

A bar called Archives, part of Oaks Hotel in Reedley, was popular with the underage drinkers, including Barney, at college. They often had live music, and one Friday a duo singing covers to backing tapes were being barracked. They had enough and walked off shouting, '*You fucking do it then, you wankers.*'

Everyone went quiet… apart from Barney, who jumped up and started belting out George Michael's 'Careless Whisper', which was next up on the backing tape. Later that evening he was approached by two lads from the year above him at college who wanted to start a band. Jez played drums, Duncan played guitar. They were looking for a singer and asked if he wanted to join them. They were thinking 'Plastic Spearmen' was a good name, because plastic spears can't hurt anyone.

Handmade A4 poster for the Mechanics

The band played their first gig a couple of months after they formed. At the Archives. No bass player, just the three of them. Barney singing and on keyboards, doing a cover of Booker T. & the M.G.s' 'Green Onions' as the intro. They proceeded to play a set of rock 'n' roll standards. The place was rammed and an enthusiastic write-up appeared in the *Burnley Express*, waxing lyrical about 16-year-old Barney Williams bringing the house down. Next time Barney went into the Archives, they refused to serve him.

Buoyed by this success they quickly expanded the band to include a bass player, two saxophonists and a trumpet player. And the set shifted to an emphasis that was more R & B, more boogie-woogie (still Barney's favourite music genre), drawing heavily on the music and clothes from *The Blues Brothers*, which Barney's brother Mark had taken him to see in 1983.

Gigs followed. The height of Plastic Spearmen's success saw them become the first band to sell out the newly refurbished and reopened Burnley Mechanics Institute on 30 July 1987. A splendid 625 people. Other than Barney, nobody who would become a Milltown Brother was there. But Jonathan Bibby was, and he would become a huge fan of the Milltown Brothers and get involved with much of their music and activity in later years – and indeed this book.

The night remains a legendary highlight of Burnley youth culture. £2 a head to get in, promoted by Barney and the band with scrawled A4 posters and a hand-painted white bedsheet in the window of an empty shop next door to the Mechanics. An upwardly mobile band from Manchester called James had played the Mechanics the week before. They were just about to release their second album and Jonathan had been there too. They'd played to just 60 people.

Part 2
FLYING (1987–1991)

'This is no new fad, it's pop with bollocks.'
Steve Lamacq

Groundwork

April 1987. Simon home from Finchley and working at Colne Library until his last hurrah with the Word Association in the south of France. To which Matthew was also invited. Match practice? The other thing he filled his time with was playing and working on songs with Matthew and James. More match practice? It was the start of their last term at school and final exams, Simon going up most weekends made sure they did even less revision. James loved it. *'Playing with Simon took me right back to the time I was learning and would get lost for hours. Time just flew – it was intuitive, electric and hypnotic for me, nothing was like it. We just played off each other and played and played. I'd call it my flow state these days.'*

Simon felt 'Salford Lady' – that first demo made by the Spire the year before – was bigger, bolder and just all round better at interpreting the fusion of Southern Gothic, Dylan and REM than he'd achieved with the Word Association. The three of them booked some studio time at Lancaster Musicians Co-op, before the south of France. Aided by a drum machine, they demoed four songs written by Simon and Matthew: 'The First Time', 'Lucy's Back in Town', 'Beautiful Young Lady' and 'An Education'.

Simon and James shared lead guitar duties and Simon played bass. No one can remember why a drum machine was preferred to Nian; the assumption is he was away on some sporting endeavour or too busy trying to pass exams. Thirty-five years later these demos appeared on the 2022 Milltown Brothers compilation *Tongue-Tied Mesmerised*. They're pleasant enough, in an earnest Bluebells meets Lloyd Cole kind of way.

On the day after Matthew's last exam, his place at Manchester Poly secure – notwithstanding a complete disaster with his results – the brothers headed off to the south of France. On stage Matthew took lead vocals on a handful of songs. U2's 'With or Without You', Tom Jones' 'It's Not Unusual', the Beatles' 'I Feel Fine'. Free from school and straight to an eternally sunny paradise beside the sea, he became a pop star. Everyone who saw the band was on a mission to have the time of their life, everyone in the band keen to help them. His teeth got cut in all manner of ways.

Come September, they were back in the north-west, eager to make more music. Matthew with a holiday hangover. Sorry, overhang. Unsubtly different from the boy who left in June. Cowboy boots, a long leather coat and rather racy neckerchief, to accompany his healthy tan, bleached blond locks… and a little balloon of attitude.

And just before Manchester Poly became home for Matthew, James and Nian, Simon booked more time at Lancaster Musicians Co-op and worked on more new demos with Matthew and James. Songs the Nelson Brothers had written in the south of France: 'Welcome to the Blue Sky', 'Clouds Over Your Eyes', 'Somewhere Between' and 'How Long?'. As with the June session, Simon and James shared lead guitar duties and Simon again played bass. Nian was again absent. Only 'Somewhere Between' made it on to the 2022 compilation, *Tongue-Tied Mesmerised*. And as Matthew, James and Nian finally descended on Manchester Poly, Simon began compiling an 8-track cassette tape of the demos from the two sessions.

The *'bit of a lost idiot'*, as Matthew describes himself, persisted in both dress sense and attitude in his first few weeks at Manchester Poly. France had been an extraordinary and exotic taste of life. This caused hilarity among his friends and disdain among strangers. Fortunately – if painfully – the anonymous girl described at the beginning of this book calling him *'a dickhead'* wasn't the only one and he quickly came to his senses.

Meanwhile Simon relocated to London to live with girlfriend Rachel and this time got a desk job hiring heavy plant machinery to North Africa – the old French colonies. He started sending out the demo tape to record companies and, to make it credible, used the name the Milltown Brothers – which he remembered Matthew mentioning at the Millionaire Brothers gig with Mark. He called the tape the suitably earthy *Songs From the Black Stone*, stuck a photo of him and Matthew on it and included a press release – complete with his brother in cowboy boots – describing them as partners. Poor James never got a mention.

'I sent it to names I knew from trying to get something going for the Word Association during 1986 and early 1987, the usual suspects and mostly record companies – MCA, Warner Bros Polydor, EMI, Phonogram – and some indies like Rough Trade. A couple got back to me saying they liked some songs but it was too early and said

That press release

we should be gigging in London. The Word Association had been a tough experience down there, but it was still part of the reason I'd moved back south even though I didn't have a clue what the shape of things would or wouldn't be with Matthew, James and Nian. But I made sure I got a job... later in 1988 Chrysalis Music got interested in us and paid for some demos. The A & R guy Bruce Craigie pulled out a copy of the Songs from the Black Stone *tape saying he'd been tracking us for a while... maybe that justified us sticking with the name. Maybe.'*

As a group of lads they couldn't believe they'd pulled off the Manchester Poly move. They were more together than ever, if not quite a band, even though Nian was in Stretford and Simon – now very much part of the gang – was in London. He drove up to Manchester every weekend in his Fiat Uno, to play (drink and carry on) with any combination of Matthew, James, Nian... and this new lad Barney they'd just met, who happened to be from Burnley, a good laugh and great keyboard player by all accounts.

Matthew had been given a place to live at Rosebank Hall in Didsbury for the first year, and James lived five minutes' walk away. Rosebank was an old house converted to student accommodation with separate purpose-built student accommodation, Greystoke Hall, in its grounds. In the whole place, there were just two rooms sharing a bathroom squeezed between them – with access from both sides. Matthew got one of those rooms.

As for Barney, he was given a place to live at Rosebank Hall too. And he got the only other room that had a shared bathroom. Ridiculous. Matthew and Barney were no longer strangers, they were intimately semi-detached neighbours, having initially bumped into each other in their shared bathroom. And it was love at first sight, despite the cowboy boots.

The band materialised a couple of months' worth of fun, games and very few lectures after Matthew and Barney met, on the evening of Friday, 4 December 1987 in the basement of Rosebank Hall. A room they found complete with – somewhat wondrously – an almost in-tune piano. And Dave Knaggs, the amenable live-in warden of the hall, was very happy for them to rehearse there. Simon (24), Matthew (19), James (19), Nian (18) and Barney (18) were now a band.

What did they have on 4 December 1987? Quite a bit at a modest level... some studio and live experience, talent, ridiculous belief, an as yet undiscovered potential for magic, brotherly love, an *all for one, and one for all* spirit, and a shared love of drinking and carrying on. They also had an already productive Nelson brother songwriting team (Nick and Max doing the dirty work), a very nice place to play (free and more or less always available), Simon living in London who knew how to get gigs, all the time in the world to practise together, probably one guitarist too many, a keyboard player they hadn't been looking for, a tape *Songs From the Black Stone* featuring three of the band under the Milltown Brothers banner – and they already believed they had some better new songs. But most important of all, they already appeared to have lots of luck.

The good fortune hung around. They enjoyed well over three years of it, managing to be in the right place at the right time on far more occasions than they were in the wrong place at the wrong time. So that spark of potential magic got plenty of encouragement. Says Barney now, '*You've got to live it just to get good and we were lucky, the shared situation we found ourselves in and our not going to any lectures to speak of, Dave Knaggs and that room. I don't see how you can do it these days without having money or support behind you, so big respect to anyone who makes something of the luck they get. We got much more time together than most people ever could've done and we got lucky straight afterwards too.*'

And just as important, the million and one things that could've gone wrong never did. Well, not in an obvious way. The most interesting was when Nian – never trust a drummer however okay he appears – might have left to drum for The La's, who the Milltown Brothers toured with a few years later. He was stuck out in Stretford in a house with a bunch of guys he didn't get on with and nothing seemed to be happening. He'd seen The La's at his Freshers gig and they were his new favourite band. Shortly afterwards their drummer left the band, and they put a phone number out on radio for anyone who fancied replacing him and Nian was listening. He hurtled barefoot to the nearest phone box and then the next until he found one that was working, but never managed to get through.

And what didn't they have? Remarkably a much shorter list. No professional help or exposure – their good fortune would quickly take care of that, no bass player and no agreement about what they were called. How these last two issues were sorted out explains a great deal about the band that was to be. For better and worse.

Bass

A couple of early auditions achieved nothing, no brothers unearthed. In the first few months of 1988 there was a bit of toing and froing between Simon and James, musical chairs in ever decreasing circles. For their first half-dozen gigs, Simon and then James played lead guitar on some demos and certain songs live, and bass on others. But James effectively took more and more of the bass work up 'temporarily', an inevitable result of the Nelson brother songwriting combo. And the unforeseen arrival of Barney and keyboards meant there wasn't much room for a second guitarist or sixth member, sonically, financially or spatially.

None of them was great at confrontation. One day James was left without a chair and the bass in his hand. It was all a bit clumsy, this switching around on stage, and they wanted to appear professional, like a proper band. That was that, even though he'd continue to contribute lead guitar as and when in the studio. But it was never actually talked about or agreed.

Simon explains, *'It was the elephant in the room sometimes. But maybe that was just me. Nobody was keen on confrontation and it didn't feel necessary anyway, so we felt our way forward. James is a better guitarist than me, more technical than me, a great player. I often felt under pressure and had to learn to play better. The fact he was there pushed me all the time, I was often wondering what he was thinking about my playing. He stood in temporarily on bass and then no one had an appetite for another addition to the band, but I think how busy we got gig-wise and demoing almost from day one was a great compensation. We were busy musicians. Whatever, it worked and he's a marvellous and brilliant bass player too. I'm not sure I can think of anyone with his dexterity and imagination. He might have been upset but never showed it and dealt with the whole thing with remarkable equanimity.'*

James has no memory of it being a big deal. Simon had already shown his willingness to pick up the bass in those early sessions but critically was more involved in the songwriting with Matthew, so it wasn't so much a decision as an unfolding. Equally it wasn't what James had been expecting at the start of term when he'd excitedly invested his grant on a Telecaster and amp. Fortunately the place he bought it from was willing to exchange it for an Ibanez bass and amp. And Barney is eternally grateful James was happy to play bass. *'He's a ridiculously melodic player, it was a massive positive for the band, a great thing and I loved watching him fall in love with it.'*

Awkward as it may appear, it's a wonderful example of the band embracing their togetherness. Common good and utilitarianism in action. And as a result, they were able to make the most of their luck for ages. No throwing out the baby with the bath water. It's what bound them – and made the brothers they claimed to be much more than marketing bollocks and a cheap target for the press. Along with all the matey stuff, they instinctively shared a kind of similar view of the world and what was important. Which is the reason the sum of the parts was so much bigger than the parts. There was harmony on and off stage, such that the greater good, achievement and fun for all far outweighed who played bass and who played guitar. Or who wrote and who didn't. Or who drove and who didn't. Or who took drugs and who didn't. Or who walked around a stage and who didn't. Underneath it all, they just wanted the best outcome for the gang and to keep the whole thing going. They knew without the gang they were nothing. And whatever it was, it was never too big a deal or a sacrifice. For anyone.

James both happy and sad

Nevertheless a couple of photos of James playing lead guitar and in an early session make entertaining viewing.

Milltown Brothers?

In many ways the band ended up being called the Milltown Brothers for the same reason James became the bass player. No one was hot on confrontation and the togetherness and harmony of the band was the most important thing of all. There was never much of a discussion and the name chose them because it was already there, courtesy of Simon sticking it on to that *Songs From the Black Stone* tape, to make them seem like a band. It was part of the furniture, the path of least resistance and no one seemed

that bothered, even though Nian claims he's always thought it was crap and implied far too much.

Simon eventually got round to attempting to empty it of any meaning in an article in the *West Lancashire Evening Gazette* in October 1990. '*It's evocative but uninspirational – people have tried to read a lot into it for the sake of their reviews and the articles about us but really it's just a name.*'

Yes, it is – and no, it's not. Whatever you think about it, the two words together bring lots of stuff – baggage, expectations and potential pitfalls: it reinforces not just their working class roots but also their roots in the north-west, with echoes of the Industrial Revolution and the idea of heroism in hard labour. Henry Giles, the nineteenth-century Irish preacher who spent three years as minister at Toxteth Park chapel, expressed it rather well. '*There is no work so rude that man may not exalt it; no work so impassive that he may not breathe a soul into it; no work so dull that he may not enliven it.*' The name also suggests kinship, heritage, a spirit that is dyed in the wool and, perhaps, backward-looking.

There's little doubt if you have a name like the Milltown Brothers and are anything vaguely unworthy or frivolous, you're asking for trouble. Imposing on yourself the need to be so damned real, down-to-earth and authentic. Past, present and future. Forever. And it frames and colours everything you do.

For an uplifting, fun-loving rock/indie band delivering *'pop with bollocks'*, who happened to like drinking, to be young, callow, quite cute enough, and with – however superficially – a northern middle-class upbringing, their name may have had some very short-term logic in relation to the *Black Stone* tape being out there… but in Thatcher's Britain, with its predatory, politicised and fickle music press, it was stupid and short-sighted.

Don't shape expectations before people even hear your music. Choose something relatively meaningless that you and your fans can define and fill with meaning over time. Like Blur, Elastica, Oasis, The La's, Belly, Slowdive, Suede, Sweet, Slade… or even Spire. But they didn't. Those reading this who've never heard of the band will already have formed an opinion of the kind of music they played and may have made similarly unfounded associations to the likes of the Luddites, *The Waltons* and *Last of the Summer Wine*.

It would be reasonable to say the success they eventually had was despite the name – and they've lived with the consequences ever since. It didn't matter when things were going well – the music blew everything away, they could brush the digs off – but when they weren't, it made them an easy target for the press. An anachronism, a marketing pretence, trying to be something they weren't, their music suddenly derivative and backward-looking rather than *'pop with bollocks'*.

When interviewed they naturally fell – or were provoked – into the incongruous habit of trying to justify themselves and defend their authenticity, all of which should have been a non-issue. An article, 'Northern Punt Rock', written by Max Bell and appearing in *Vox*, August 1991, is fronted by a picture of the band punting on the River Cam in Cambridge, with a leader that reads: '*Caught boating in the seat of learning, a well-known*

Northern punt rockers

northern band deny their cloth cap, ferret-trousered heritage.' It quotes Barney: *'We've all had crap jobs. Matthew worked in a sewer digging shit out of blocked pipes. Nian's been a packer in an ice cream factory. I've worked in a bottling factory painting palettes* [sic].'

The band had an early and ugly indication of the trouble the name could cause – and it came from a completely different direction. They played their seventh-ever gig on 6 May 1988 at the New Pegasus in Stoke Newington, supporting the Irish band Energy Orchard.

Just a month or so earlier, Northern Ireland had witnessed one of the most traumatic sequences of violence in the history of the troubles. Three IRA members were shot dead in Gibraltar by the SAS in highly controversial and disputed circumstances. The three became instant martyrs and their coffins were returned to Belfast, where the route to the cemetery was lined with thousands of mourners.

During their burial a lone loyalist gunman launched an attack on the mourners, killing three. One of those killed was a member of the IRA, and at his subsequent funeral at the same cemetery two British army corporals inexplicably drove their car into the cortège. It was besieged. Though armed, the corporals were overwhelmed, dragged from the car, beaten and eventually shot dead. Most of this was captured on TV.

Unfortunately, the name of the cemetery where this all took place was Milltown and the band they were supporting had strong Republican sympathies. Energy Orchard took offence after events so brutal and raw, apparently resenting being associated with a brotherhood of sorts. The band walked innocently into a hail of scorn and aggression and spent an uncomfortable evening protesting their innocence of extreme loyalist sympathies. They weren't even fully aware of what had gone on. It was a dreadful alignment of events – and still they kept the name. Although, to be fair, it was too late to do anything about it. The week before the Energy Orchard gig, they'd got lucky: they'd bumped into Steve Lamacq.

Steve Lamacq

The band were quick off the mark. Their first demo session took place at the Lancaster Musicians Co-op, on 19 December 1987, just over two weeks after they'd formed. *Songs From the Black Stone* might be out there, but Nian and Barney weren't, or James really. And they were ready to do better.

They demoed four songs: 'Ocean Fields', 'Helplessly', 'Tyrant's Name' and Australia Day. 'Ocean Fields', a reworked version of a song Simon wrote with the Word Association, remains part of the band's live set to this day, while 'Australia Day' is reputedly Matthew's most disliked Milltown Brothers' song – certainly not among the 50 or so he's described as being *'our favourite song'* over 35 years. This session would be central to them getting a publishing deal with EMI. All four tracks turned up on the *Tongue-Tied Mesmerised* compilation in 2022.

They played their first gig a couple weeks later in January 1988, in the canteen of Greystoke Hall, next door to where Matthew and Barney lived, at the beginning of the new term.

All four songs from their first session got an airing, plus half of the *Songs From the Black Stone*, and Barney sang 'Brand New Cadillac', a UK rock 'n' roll classic originally by Vince Taylor and His Playboys, covered by the Clash on *London Calling*.

Simon in rather un-rock 'n 'roll fashion considerately halted proceedings mid-song to hold up a bunch of keys that had been handed in and asked if anyone had lost them.

He soon redeemed himself, managing to arrange a few gigs in and around London in the weeks that followed, and the other 80 per cent of the band plus Nick and/or Max began to get into the habit of setting off from Manchester when they were ready – usually too late, and hurtling down to a pub somewhere around London, meeting a harassed and marginally panicky Simon with no time to do a soundcheck, quickly setting up and playing. Despite which, they say they never missed a gig. And then they drove back north the same night – all in a Salford Hire van. Apart from once, in Matthew's mum's car, with the band squeezed in among the gear, though they had to sacrifice Nick.

Their fifth London gig – and sixth in total – a week before the Energy Orchard gig, was at a grim and near deserted Hype Club in the Bull & Gate in Kentish Town on 29 April 1988. They were the first of five bands on. Bottom of an awful bill, but very lucky.

Andrew Collins tells the story in *NME*, 'Milltown Brats', 26 May 1990: '*The Milltowns played their jumpy, furrow-browed pop set to 11 people. "But there was this one guy on the left really getting into it!" And who was that masked man? The ever-masochistic Steve Lamacq. Cue. The Big Time... Or maybe not.*'

Yes, that Steve Lamacq, then of the *NME* and later Radio 1 and champion of undiscovered talent. Also writing in *NME*, in September 1990, he explains: '*I've got fate to thank for this one. Imagine it's Friday you've just been to London's Town & Country Club to see the first band on and you've left early to catch something on TV. Then just as you're passing the Bull & Gate, that dim-lit stop-off in Kentish Town, a little voice starts nagging away in your head... 'check out the back room, check out the back room'... The good group, four songs into their set, looked cute but commanding; five slightly shy boys down from the north making up for their lack of experience with a rigorous charm that you couldn't fault. But more than that, this group, who the sound engineer told me were called the MILLTOWN BROTHERS, had something extra. Their pop songs were harder than other people's, their rock songs were less pompous. With a dash of forceful harmonies and some tricky guitar lines to boot, woven through their combustible set, The Milltown Brothers first proper gig had that flaming sparkle of Big Things To Come.'*

After the show Steve introduced himself, asked if they had a demo tape, told them there'd be a review in *NME*. Was he taking the piss?

Clearly not. No other band from the gig was mentioned. Every silver lining usually has a cloud, but not this one. Following Steve's review their gigs in London were suddenly much better attended. Mostly with A & R scouts, execs from various record companies and the music press. *NME* colleagues Andrew Collins and Iestyn George, Nick Duerden at *Record Mirror* and Dave Simpson at *Melody Maker* – despite editorial reticence – were just some of the writers that became supporters of the band... well before the Milltown Brothers' first birthday.

Caroline Elleray

Caroline Elleray had just started her first job fresh from college at Strawberry Studios. At around the same time as the gig at the Bull & Gate, James had jumped on a bus to Stockport to visit an aunt and uncle who lived there, a couple of streets away from Strawberry Studios. Members of 10cc founded and part-owned this place until the mid-80s. Paul McCartney, the Ramones, the Smiths, Happy Mondays, Joy Division and, of course, 10cc are a few of the bands who've recorded there. James did something uncharacteristically plucky and took along a tape of the first demos the band had recorded in December, aiming to call in. More characteristically, he didn't tell anyone in the band he was going.

He can remember three things about his visit. Firstly, being intimidated and excited in equal measure by the multitude of precious metal discs festooning the walls. Secondly being greeted by Caroline, who he describes as a wonderfully warm, engaging, dynamic, interested and interesting young woman. And thirdly 10cc's 'The Things We Do For Love' – created there in 1977 – playing on the peerless sound system. He describes it as *a thing of majesty and perfection* and he's welcome to his opinion.

Caroline was ambitious and, despite not having much of a clue about how things worked, looking to launch an independent record label. What she heard on James' tape convinced her the Milltown Brothers were the people to help her do it. One or two phone calls later (easy to say in six words but nowhere near as easy in those days as it would be today), a meeting or two with her boss – and suddenly the band had people taking them seriously and wanting to help. They were on the road to launching Big Round Records with a bit of a champion in Caroline.

When they started using the studio, the Happy Mondays were there during the day recording and remixing their second album *Bummed*, with Martin Hannett producing. The Milltown Brothers loved the stories of gross excess and shenanigans relayed to them during their visits. It didn't frame their expectations of what real bands did for kicks, but you know.

They ended up doing seven sessions at Strawberry – four in downtime overnight – mostly with John Pennington, a young Youth Training Scheme (YTS) sound engineer, assisted by Jonathan Barrett. Now based in LA, John has since worked with an array of artists including New Order, Moby, Röyksopp and Run the Jewels. John was clearly an astonishing YTS success story (at a time when these were few and far between).

Looking back, Nian says, *'I don't think we legally signed anything with Big Round Records. It was more a case of them just helping us out and wanting to start a label using one of our songs. As I remember, it was all done on a trust basis, but I could be wrong. After James initially went to drop the demo tape off, we went in and recorded with their YTS engineer John Pennington, so it may have*

John and the band overnight at Strawberry

been a case of him wanting to get his teeth into something and us being in the right place at the right time. It was a buzz being in a "real" 24-track studio...if a little daunting. We'd start around 8 p.m. and work through until the morning. A great experience and learning curve.'

The band did sign an agreement with Big Round Records/Strawberry Studios, but the label went on to release just three singles, including two by the Milltown Brothers. The terms were quite loose and there was no long-term vision.

'Janice Is Gone' was the first demo the band recorded in June 1988. This was the song Matthew and Simon wrote about DJ Janice Long's exit from Radio 1, as a result of Simon meeting her briefly at Rock City in Nottingham and by the banks of the Leeds and Liverpool canal in 1984. It was the band's first public release, part of the *Manchester North of England* 14-track compilation cassette issued later in 1988, featuring among others the

Man from Delmonte, Inspiral Carpets, James and the Railway Children. The tape become central in the mythology surrounding the explosion of the Madchester scene, and the Milltown Brothers were caught in the light.

This was followed by a session in July producing 'We've Got Time' and 'Something On My Mind' and one in August where they demoed 'Roses'. These were part-funded by Chrysalis, who were the first label to take serious notice of the band with the *Songs From the Black Stone* tape. These three tracks, with 'Roses' as the lead, would become the band's first single and Big Round Records' first release – *Coming From The Mill* – in April 1989.

Their next session took place in October 1988 and produced 'Silver Town' and 'Why Should I' with the additional input of London-based producer Harold Burgon. These would become the B-sides of Big Round Records third and final release – and the Milltown Brothers' second single – 'Which Way Should I Jump?' in October 1989.

Their first daytime session and last of 1988 was in November and resulted in 'Tomorrow', paid for by Electra and produced by Jonathan Barrett. 'Tomorrow' is something of a mystery, a fondly remembered lost song; no one close to the band has a copy and no one can get anywhere near remembering exactly how it went.

Two more sessions were to take place at Strawberry Studios. The first of these was in July 1989. After the initial demoing of 'Which Way Should I Jump?' at EMI studios in June (along with 'Sitting In The Shade') it was recorded at Strawberry at this session, with new producer Chris Allison.

Following the signing of their recording deal with A&M in March 1990, the band's next – and last – session at Strawberry Studios took place overnight between 3 and 4 April 1990. Produced by John Pennington, who was no longer YTS, it was a thing of wonder. The outputs were the first versions of 'Apple Green', 'Don't Breathe In' and 'We're Doing Fine'. All these songs would feature in different ways in the making of their first album *Slinky*, although you'll find only 'Apple Green' among the song titles. Nick particularly remembers this session, or at least the first few hours. It was his 21st birthday and the band helped him celebrate all night, which in turn helped them produce some magic.

Caroline has gone on to have a hugely successful career in the music industry. Eleven years after James popped into Strawberry Studios, she was instrumental in Coldplay signing to Parlophone in April 1999 and still works with them today. There's a nice coincidence here: Steve Lamacq helped Coldplay too. Three months before signing with Parlophone, they became the first unsigned band to do a session on his Radio 1 show.

What the two did for the Milltown Brothers was huge, giving them exposure, studio time and a chance. Very early on. They had no management, no booking agent, no regular crew, no publishing deal and no recording contract. Just Nick and Max helping out and Simon arranging gigs. They needed help.

Tim Paton

Tim Paton knew Steve Lamacq. He was a photographer at *NME* – tough work in the days before digital. There was the need to get a decent shot in just a few clicks of the camera, then develop film the same night – and deliver prints or a contact sheet with the images ASAP to the *NME* picture editor at a time with no email. And he was paid – not very much – on the size of image, if they used a shot at all. It usually cost him more to produce than he was paid. Which is why he needed a second job in the music business alongside the photography.

Tim had already got lucky. He'd started working life with an HND in Business Studies and a dogsbody job his dad got him at Tindle Newspapers, which produced both *Haslemere Herald* and *Farnham Herald*. Then the paper's photographer walked out. Tim liked taking photos in his spare time and knew how to develop film. He got the job… One day in the office, someone mentioned that the Monkees were getting ready to play that evening in the pub next door. This was 1987, 20 years after the Monkees' heyday in America, and it wasn't 1 April. Tim went to have a look, just in case, and found Davy Jones and Peter Tork setting up with a backing band. He sold a photo to *Melody Maker*. Crazy.

It got crazier. He blagged a meeting at the *NME* and was showing his portfolio of mostly local Haslemere and Farnham bands to the picture editor. The phone rang, a photographer crying off. The next thing he was on his way to see That Petrol Emotion at the Town & Country Club in Kentish Town as *NME*'s photographer, and he didn't have a clue who they were. A career was born.

Tim then got himself the chance of that second job in the music industry at Globeshine band management, with Brian Hallin who looked after the Wedding Present. All he needed was to find a band, and Steve Lamacq told him about the Milltown Brothers and his newly defined genre, pop with bollocks. The next time they played the Bull & Gate, Tim was there taking photos; he loved them and was first in the queue after the show, all boundless enthusiasm and no band management experience whatsoever. And he was 24, younger than Simon.

The band were excited and desperate. They liked Tim, liked the fact he liked them, and they liked the Wedding Present. Only Barney was unsure. He felt they had nothing to compare Tim with and was expecting their manager to be a tough single-minded, ruthless Svengali, like Led Zeppelin's Peter Grant, who shouldn't be trying to do two jobs. Tim was persuasive and so the band once more found the easiest solution to a problem right in front of them, they didn't need to go looking – the path of least resistance.

Within a few weeks they'd signed a four-year management deal. Tim had his band and his other job. Globeshine had 20 per cent of everything and taking photographs remained his second job. What could possibly go wrong? Nothing, everything was going their way. '*We were all young, making it up as we went along, you don't understand it was bloody chaos,*' says Tim now.

He began to sort stuff out, but they didn't see much of Brian. And when they did, he didn't much remind them of Peter Grant (or what they imagined Peter Grant to be like). Tim got them a booking agent first in autumn 1988: Concorde and the *'lovely, tireless'* John Gammon. His brief was simple: Get the Milltown Brothers playing wherever and whenever you can.

The band got a reputation for doing it tirelessly. And increasingly brilliantly, often better than the band they were supporting. *'The Milltown Brothers are one of those finds. Supporting diabolically stagnant indie bands, this five piece from various parts of Lancashire played a set of songs so strong in passion and conviction that their supposed superiors must have felt ashamed to share a stage with them,' wrote* Ron Rom, reviewing Dingwalls, Camden for *Sounds*, January 1989.

Nian continues the story. *'Tim Paton mentioned that we'd been offered the support on The La's tour, but it was going to cost a few thousand to get on it. I remember taking him aside and unlike me, being quite insistent he made it happen. It did and I got to see my favourite band live every night for 15 dates. Interestingly we were flying and half the audience was ours. We were more dynamic live and in danger of blowing them away each night. They watched nervously from the side as their support band went down a storm. They raised their game, and their originality probably won the day.'*

For the *Guardian*, 14 March 1991, Bruce Dessau wrote: *'Most bands who tour as the support act rarely upstage the star turn... The Milltown Brothers have latterly outpointed The La's, whom they play with this weekend...'*

During 1988 the band played at least 18 gigs, including the Marquee where Jesus danced. By the time of their last gig of the year at the Camden Palace in London, Tim had got a publishing deal with EMI; the 'Ocean Fields' demos alongside a Strawberry Studios tape featuring 'Something On My Mind', 'Janice Is Gone' and 'We've Got Time' were instrumental in the process. The band signed the deal on 1 December 1988 and got a £25,000 advance. Not only would the gig that evening at the Camden Palace be their last of the year, it would be the last they played as students – or, in Simon's case, while being gainfully employed elsewhere. They were now going full-time.

But the first impact of the deal – other than sheer elation and a brilliant gig – was that 80 per cent of the band did their best to die in a car crash. Matthew was especially good at nearly dying, which would have been a problem. But they got lucky. The band minus Simon had spent all day celebrating in the Bierkeller Manchester with Barney's mate Will. They arrived in Will's car and unwisely left in his car, then drove through a crossroads at speed. Another car hit them at speed, just where Matthew was sitting by the rear passenger door. Instead of being killed instantly, Matthew nutted Nian, knocking him unconscious, on the way out of the window of the car, corpse-style, facing the sky, as it spun over. He ended up unconscious in the road, but somehow both cars and the road missed him, and he landed as if on a bed of air. The rest of them were still in the car and miraculously unhurt, other than Nian's headache. Matthew eventually walked to hospital, stopping for a burger on the way, and other than mild concussion there was nothing wrong with him. Will emigrated to Canada shortly after.

The second impact of the deal was they could afford to buy themselves some better instruments and a van. A bright orange Ford Transit joined the band.

And the third was that they could go full-time and started to pay themselves a salary of sorts, £400 a month each. They left Manchester Poly before they were thrown out and Simon stopped wearing a suit and tie.

Coming From The Mill

In April 1989 the band released their first single while playing and planning more and more gigs. After a warm-up at the Square in Harlow on 9 April, they played a 15-date tour of the UK in support of *Coming From The Mill*, starting at Aberystwyth University on 21 April and closing with their first gig at the Town & Country Club in Kentish Town on 26 May. *Coming From The Mill* was the first of four singles released over the next two years, paving the way towards the expected big hit with the release of the fifth, 'Here I Stand'. This makes it sound like a carefully considered plan. It wasn't. 'Material World', *NME*, April 1991 recorded this exchange: *'Biggest misconception about you?' 'That we know what we are doing.'*

Big Round Records first release appeared on 7" vinyl with 'Roses' and 'We've Got Time' and 12" vinyl and 3" CD (yes really!) with 'Roses', 'Something On My Mind' and 'We've Got Time'. All of the songs are very good – indeed, amazingly so for a first release. The Milltown Brothers would continue to issue an excellent standard of B-sides and additional tracks throughout their career.

'Roses'

> *My hometown has been turned down and there's nothing I*
> *   can do,*
> *From where I stand I see this land disappearing from my*
> *   view,*
> *Oh Stanley's lost his cap,*
> *Yeah we're all real sad about that, it's a shame.*
>
> *And who you gonna sell our roses to,*
> *Who you gonna sell 'em to,*
> *Give me something new.*
>
> *My hometown's looking out for itself, that's all it can do,*
> *Betty gets washing to make her living, at the corner shop she*
> *   spends what she's given.*
> *And Stanley lost his cap,*
> *Yeah we're all real sad about that, it's true.*
>
> *And who you gonna sell our roses to,*
> *Who you gonna sell 'em to,*
> *It's not me, it's nothing new.*

He's looking at the town which he should have left
He's lost his looks and now he's lost his health,
He's staying inside 'cos he's scared of getting wet,
Remembering the things that he hoped he'd forget,
You know he's been living his life down on the dole,
Taking low fibre diets
Getting high on cholesterol,
High on cholesterol.
There's nothing, there's nothing we can do.

And who you gonna sell your roses to,
Who you gonna sell 'em to
And who you gonna sell your roses to,
Who you gonna sell 'em to.

'Roses' is an energetic melodic threnody to the loss of northern communities following the decline of the cotton and coal industries. Serious stuff for Matthew. As such it doubled down on their northern working-class credentials. And having stuck with the Milltown Brothers name, they jumped in with both feet. For better or worse. Called the single 'Coming From The Mill' rather than 'Roses' and put the LS Lowry painting of the same name on the sleeve. They extracted a stooped working-class character from the painting as a logo for the band and included a photo by Tim with the band as modern-day ragamuffins on the cobbled streets of Colne, *'Like extras from* Last of the Summer Wine,*'* as Andrew Collins inaccurately suggested in *NME* in 1989. And in warm northern fashion they thanked all manner of people, including Andrew the Farmer and the Bouncy, Bouncy Bouncer on the reverse.

There was even a video filmed for 'Roses'. A performance of the song in the splendid – and empty – Hippodrome Theatre in Colne. Interspersed with suitably faux antiquated black and white footage of the band stomping around Colne. This mix of band performance cut with them doing something else, usually silly, set a trend for their future videos. And *Melody Maker*

Modern day ragamuffins

delivered a scathing attack on the band's retro northern industrial imagery and limited imagination, culminating in the splendid line: *'Have you never heard of your man De Chirico?'*.

While it didn't make single of the week in *NME* (whatever Wikipedia may say), 'Roses' did receive a great review from Andrew Collins, together with a follow-up piece in *NME* a month later.

During the May tour they played a gig at the Venue in Cardiff. Backstage before the gig their support band were listening to Radio 1 and 'Roses' came on. It was the first time the Milltown Brothers heard themselves on the radio.

'Which Way Should I Jump?'

In October 1989 the Milltown Brothers' second single and Big Round Records' third and last release arrived on 7" with B-side 'Silver Town' and 12" vinyl with 'Silver Town' and 'Why Should I'. The first expression of perhaps the band's most well-known song, dealing with the frustrations and paradoxes inherent in love and relationships. Despite its self-evident loveliness, getting the song released had not been easy. Simon explains: *'Strawberry was on the cusp of not releasing 'Which Way Should I Jump?' because of rising costs in production and distribution issues and I remember driving there in the van late one afternoon with Matthew and "haranguing" the MD vigorously, persuading them to have faith in us. They did eventually put it out and it massively helped us going forward, so we are hugely grateful to them, but we had to fight for it too.'*

'Which Way Should I Jump'

Well I came up to see the sunrise,
Found myself just laying down in your eyes,
Trying hard to reach inside of your mind,
Stay with me and I'll change things in your life,

But you look like you don't care,
You stammer and you swear.

Which way should I jump?
Which way should I jump?
Which way should I jump with you?

Well I don't need to see you social,
I say I do but that's a lie
I'm taught to.

Lying by your side,
Tongue-tied mesmerised I try.

Which way should I jump?
Which way should I jump?
Which way should I jump with you?

The weather is in disarray,
Like all the things I've seen today,
Come on take me away,

Oh is it the clothes you wear,
The colour of your hair
Or your eyes they shine and shine and shine.

Which way should I jump?
Which way should I jump?
Which way should I jump with you?

Learn about the weather from the clouds

Which way should I jump?
Which way should I jump?
Which way should I jump?
Which way should I jump?

To the sky she said,
I love the colour of your hair,
To the sky she said,
Next time I swear I'll take a weather check.

Nick Morrell had heard the band working on 'Which Way Should I Jump?' for the first time on 8 June 1989 at Lancaster Musicians Co-op and knew it was special. Remarkably specific, you may think, but later the same day he went to the Sugarhouse in Lancaster with the band to watch the Stone Roses, a month or so after the release of their eponymous album, which became one of the most influential British pop/rock albums ever made. Initially peaking at 32 in the album chart, it eventually sold four million copies worldwide. Not huge, huge but hugely influential. It was the first of two paradigm-changing pop/rock albums released during the ascending arc of the parabola that was the Milltown Brothers career, and despite the odd unhelpful comparison suggesting the album instantly dated the Milltown Brother's sound, it had a positive influence on their music and prospects, putting the spotlight firmly on the north-west and guitar-driven, chiming and big-hearted melodies.

'Which Way Should I Jump?' was demoed a couple of weeks later at EMI studios and finally recorded at Strawberry Studios in July. Chris Allison was brought in as producer for both sessions – working with John Pennington – having produced the Wedding Present, management stablemates of the Milltown Brothers. The expectation was that he'd beef up the sound and, unsurprisingly, he introduced Simon and his guitar to the Marshall Stack, as 'patented' by Pete Townsend and John Entwistle in the days when it did make a difference. The blueprint for the Milltown Brothers sound was complete. Listen to 'Which Way Should I Jump?' alongside B-sides 'Silver Town' and 'Why Should I'– the first of which is an excellent song in its own right in a Deacon Blue kind of way and both of which were recorded at an earlier session – and Chris's impact and the influence of the Stone Roses is evident.

Despite not selling enough to bother the charts, it was *NME* single of the week and was played on Radio 1. You do wonder with more effective distribution and promotional support whether this could have been the making of Big Round Records and Caroline. It is, after all, a wonderful, timeless song, in many ways bearing comparison with The La's 'There She Goes'.

Then where would we have been?

After a warm-up at Manchester University on 6 September, the band played a 37-date tour of the UK in support of 'Which Way Should I Jump?' starting in Birmingham on 30 September and ending in Swansea towards the end of November. The latter date was part of six that, unusually for touring bands, took them across South Wales – visiting Cardiff, Newport, Lampeter,

Aberystwyth and Treforest. Given the criticisms of the parochial, backward-looking nature of the band's name, it's ironic that they would play their first gig in Colne only in the summer of 1990, and in Burnley another 18 months after that.

A&M

After the first two singles the Milltown Brothers finally signed a major record deal in March 1990, almost two years after they'd first been spotted by Steve Lamacq at the Bull & Gate. Strangely Tim can remember only one deal ever being on the table, but there were two. From Atlantic as well as A&M. No ifs or buts, the A&M offer was a nice financial one; they'd decided at Oxford Polytechnic in October they wanted to sign the band. Tim

Matthew contemplates his new masters

agreed an £100,000 advance for an album plus an option on a second album; the clear intention was to invest in the band and recoup quickly, which would require big singles sales alongside the album, and the label could see they had the singles. This wasn't the band's original plan, but the money was both flattering and enticing. A year or so after they signed, Matthew appeared perfectly happy with what was going on. He told *Vox*, April 1991 ('Brothers in Psalms'), *'Although it's a worry when you join a major, that they're going to stitch you up, so far so good. They're really excited about us, we're a fresh band for them. And they haven't put any pressure on us to have hits.'* Significantly the interview took place when the Milltown Brothers couldn't put a foot wrong, around the time of the release of *Slinky* and just before 'Here I Stand' was released.

Maybe the deal wasn't right for them. They'd always been focused on developing slowly as an albums band, like REM. They wouldn't have had things differently, but in many ways both Steve and Caroline had changed things dramatically for them too soon. Giving them early exposure and the opportunity to make a single or two. Which they were patently good at.

The band were chuffed to bits by all this, but unbalanced. Things were now much less clear than they had once been. The plan to build a sustainable career like REM with strong albums that slowly percolated into the public domain was hijacked by circumstance. Success. Money. Fame. What could be more distracting?

And there was the other offer. From Atlantic Records based in New York: a six-album deal with a £10,000 advance. Obviously the advance was 10 times less than the A&M offer, but that and the six-album deal suggested they'd commit to the band, spend less recording the albums, do it in a far more efficient, organic, 'live' way and get new music out regularly, which would have suited the band and given them much more autonomy. And crucially Atlantic wouldn't have expected such an immediate large return on their investment, giving them even more latitude and a greater life expectancy.

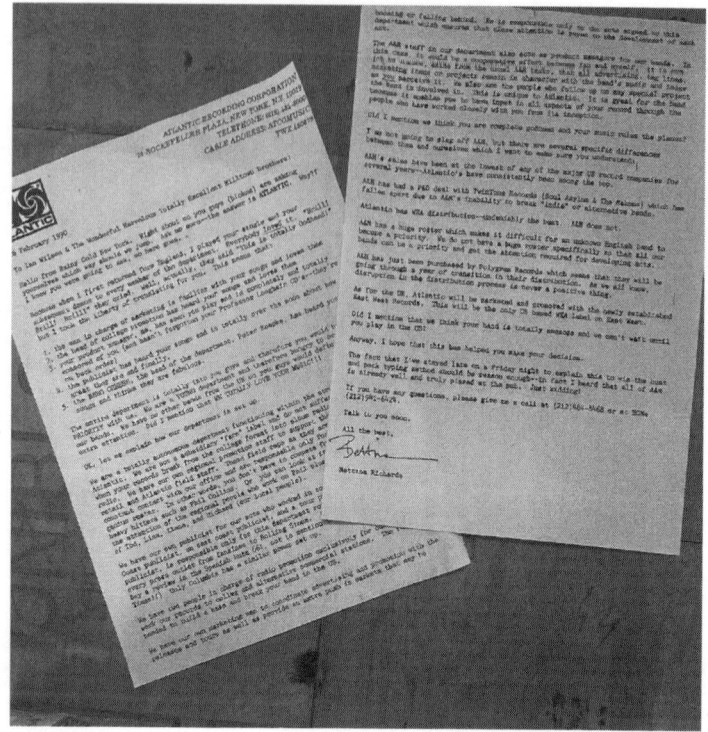

That wonderful, marvellous fax

The band were genuinely torn. Both labels had a great roster of artists, including Ray Charles, Otis Redding, Yes and Led Zeppelin in the case of Atlantic, and the Carpenters, Sex Pistols (for a week), the Police and Bryan Adams on A&M. There's no doubt Barney's head was turned by the Atlantic catalogue, but A&M was seen as a more relevant contemporary label with an indie guitar band-sized gap in their roster. Not that Atlantic didn't have a gap too.

Atlantic were persuaded to significantly uplift their advance, but Tim and Globeshine were emphatically supportive of the offer from A&M – and Howard Berman, Head of A&M, declared his love for the band. On the other hand, the *Wonderful*

Marvellous Totally Excellent Milltown Brothers...' received a fax from the staff at Atlantic on 16 February 1990 as they wrestled with the decision.

It was close. By way of a 3 to 2 vote the band decided to go with A&M. Sean O' Sullivan was the A & R guy responsible for completing the deal on A&M's behalf. *'Sean was a strange one,'* says Simon. *'At first, even though he brought us into A&M, we were always a little bit stand-offish with him and he was with us. And that wasn't like us, it was weird. Maybe because he was around to make sure we were spending A&M's money "wisely", we were a bit wary. Maybe we could have embraced the whole idea of A&M with a bit more heart and soul rather than thinking somehow because they were this giant record company we were in some strange dance with them – it all comes down to trust and it came back to bite us in the end, but we never felt wanted or special. Over time Sean kind of became part of the team – quite literally when we played in five-a-side football competitions... no great comfort now, but when James [the band] were beating us in the charts we were wupping them at football, we always got our priorities right.'*

With the benefit of hindsight, the band feel this was probably the wrong decision. The first of a few – if you don't count the band name – but much easier to understand than the ones which came later. No one knows what would have happened if they'd chosen Atlantic; it might have been a disaster. This was their choice and they were in it together, even though there were clearly vested interests among those advising them. It was just another moment, and for quite some time things did just kept getting better.

'Seems To Me'

'Seems To Me' is perhaps the most polarising of the Milltown Brothers singles. In many ways it was a bridge between their indie past and the major future. Even though the band were signed to A&M, it was released on one of their subsidiary labels, Orca/ Suburban, and promoted as the band's last independent release,

Nigel Wood

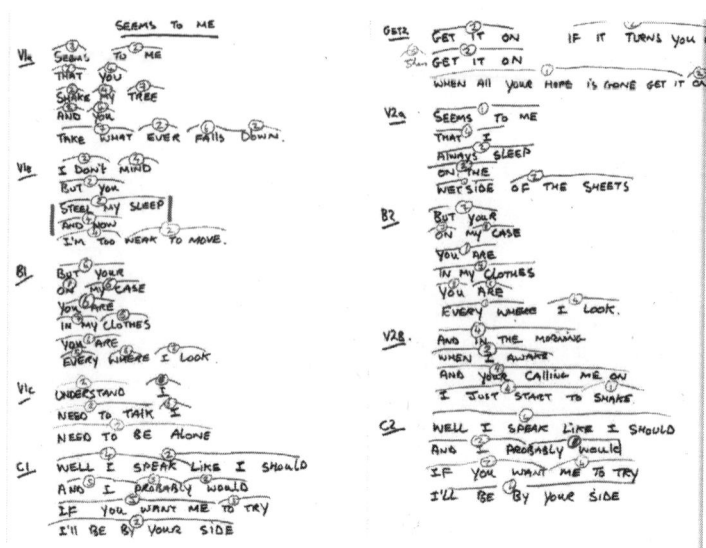

Handwritten lyrics with rehearsal notes

in May 1990. It was originally demoed at a session in London during December 1989, which also produced 'Something Cheap' and 'Natural'.

If 'Which Way Should I Jump?' had demonstrated the more subtle influence of the Stone Roses, 'Seems To Me' – backed on 7" by the equally organ festooned 'Natural', and with the addition of a dramatically loose psychedelic remix of the title track on 12" and CD – now took it a step or two further, beginning to get it on with the Happy Mondays while retaining the guitar-riff edge.

In 1991, Steve Lamacq wrote 'The Milltown Brothers Story So Far…': *'It was their second single which showed the band's strengths to the full. 'Which Way Should I Jump?' was where the urgency of new pop mixed with the warmth of Dylan-esque vocals in a rich sound that far outshone 1989's mainstream contemporaries… Into 1990 and they released their third single 'Seems To Me'. One of the highlights of their live set, it didn't quite compute on vinyl, standing alone out of context – particularly as its keyboard inspired dance swirls suggested a hint of the neighbouring Manc scally dance crossover that was erupting in the music weeklies.'*

But at the same time *Record Mirror* made it their single of the week. It did nothing but put the merest dent in the charts, and by the time of their next studio sessions looking towards the first album – and A&M single release – the band had parted company with Chris Allison and were working with Irish producer Dave Meegan. He'd been engineer during the making of U2's *The Joshua Tree* and subsequently produced most of the tracks on the eponymous debut album of House of Love. Both were admired by the Milltown Brothers.

An 18-date UK tour to support the release of 'Seems To Me', with a warm-up at University of London Union (ULU) in London on 6 April, began at the Arts Centre in Salisbury on 3 May and ended at the Charlotte in Leicester on the 26th. Their audiences were continuing to grow, as were the venues.

'Apple Green'

The first official single on A&M in October 1990, 'Apple Green' was intended as a 'soft' release – i.e. toe in the water, see what happens, evaluate the situation. It was issued on 7" backed with an early version of 'When It Comes' and on 12" vinyl and CD with the additional track 'My Favourite Place'. 'When It Comes' in this original form is very much from the same place as 'Seems To Me'. By the time it appeared as the opening track on the band's second album *Valve* in 1993, it had been transformed into an anthemic rocker.

'Apple Green'

*I'm apple green born in a field surrounded by trees
And every day in my way I try to succeed.*

*So call me apple green,
Call me apple green.*

I'm apple red a thoroughbred yet to be shared,
So on my own I applaud my self esteem.

So call me apple red,
Call me apple red.

And if you find you don't know
You've changed your mind
When you find you don't know.

I'm apple green sowing seeds and born to be free
And if they grow you might even understand me.

And call me apple green,
Call me apple green,
Call me apple green,
Call me apple green,
'Cos I'm apple green,
'Cos I'm apple green.

'Apple Green' is another uplifting tune in what can be confidently called the classic Milltown Brothers mode. A wonderful pop song, it got to 82 in the charts, which is just about what was expected from a soft release.

It was also the first Milltown Brothers release to be accompanied by a video (notwithstanding the splendid 'Roses' film). This took place among some standing stones in the Wiltshire countryside and features a collage of cuts with large white panels being carried rather frantically through the landscape by the band (an echo of the Monkees and a hint of the Banana Splits too) and the band playing against the backdrop of the white panels in the landscape. It also shows them treading on a large number of fallen apples. The contrast between the environment for this and that of the 'Roses' video is striking. It's more or less the same idea – the band playing / the band mooching around doing something else. One is vintage, the other emphatically post-modern in a Monkees/Banana Splits way. One seems to take itself seriously, the other doesn't – an interesting shift given the ongoing concerns with the Milltown Brothers as the message.

This, alongside the lyrics and images of umbrellas on the cover of the single, creates a mesh of complexity, especially as the words are arguably the most open to interpretation, meaningless and random in the Matthew Nelson cannon. Brief investigation suggests the idea might amount to innocence/beauty represented by green apples and experience/corruption by red although it is difficult to understand how the imagery supports this.

The critics lined up to offer their praises:

'Ex-Manchester Polytechnic Students in rather good record shock! Though the sleeve may be smothered in umbrellas this is the sunniest single of the fortnight. A Michael Stipe-type vocal, chiming guitars, a dash of organ and a parping chorus creates truly colourful pop. Lubricate your bedroom walls with it now.' Johnno, *Pulp*, November 1990

'Despite providing possibly the year's best single with 'Seems To Me' the public remained both unconvinced and largely unaware of the band's existence. But this is not the way of their new release 'Apple Green'. This has somehow gained airplay and acknowledgement from the all-important Auntie Beeb, with even the elderly Simon Bates and Dave Lee Travis spinning said disc. Wonders will never cease.' Nick Duerden, *What's On*, October 1990

'Britain's answer to REM have come up with a tightly wrapped, thoughtful pop parcel and the ozone-friendly guitar work is a dream. Crunchy as a Granny Smith and destined to take a big bite at the charts.' Robin Smith, *Record Mirror*, November 1990.

During the summer and autumn, the band had been record-ing their first album with Dave Meegan in Bath and London. The release of 'Apple Green' – from these sessions, not the last Strawberry Studios session on Nick Morrell's 21st birthday – and the supporting UK tour were both planned assuming the album would be complete by October. As is the way with these things, that didn't end up happening, but the album was put to one side while the band hit the road yet again for the 23-date 'Apple Green' tour beginning in Sunderland on 6 October and ending at the Fleece and Firkin in Bristol on 4 November. The band rounded the year off with two dates at the Town & Country Club in Kentish Town and a gig at the Powerhaus in Islington on 28 December.

At the second of these Town & Country gigs, they were supporting Edwyn Collins. REM weren't touring in the UK at the time, but Peter Buck and Michael Stipe were in town and had been persuaded to check the Milltown Brothers out. Things started to go wrong when an inebriated Matthew three songs in decided to speak: *'Up and coming bands like us shouldn't be supporting has-beens.'* Unsurprisingly Edwyn Collins – just the wrong side of 30 – replied in kind later in the evening. But worse had already happened. Barney emphatically ensured the band didn't get to meet REM – or pick up the support slot on their next tour. Peter Buck and Michael Stipe were waiting in the wings to say hello, Barney was the first person to step off the stage and still didn't know who REM were. Peter Buck approached him. Barney responded with; *'Piss, fart, nipple, poo…these things remind me of you.'* By the time the rest of the band got off stage, REM were no longer there.

'Which Way Should I Jump?' Revisited

The band's second official release on A&M in January 1991 was also the second release of 'Which Way Should I Jump?'. This was a new recording from the sessions for *Slinky*, overseen by Dave Meegan and remixed by Bob Kraushaar. It's regarded as the definitive version, other than all the brilliant ones those who were lucky enough to be around at the time heard live. Did the band ever truly reproduce their live sound in the studio? They don't think so, but this got close.

In addition to the 7" vinyl backed by 'Diplomat', there were a plethora of additional tracks on other formats. The 12" vinyl also included 'Knives and Forks' and 'Drop Out'; the CD included 'Drop Out' and 'Natural'; and a limited edition of 10" vinyl, 'Natural' and 'Silver Town'. In a change from the Big Round Records release, 'Which Way Should I Jump?' was credited as written by Matthew and Simon only.

The video that accompanied it continued the now familiar format of cuts of the band playing the song (variously against a black/white background) interspersed with something else going on involving the band. In this instance a black-and-white film of what initially appears to be a Matthew as Humpty Dumpty scenario. It unfolds to become the band jumping, falling or diving off an old stone harbour wall into the sea below, and then swimming around for a bit. It's not a complicated interpretation. The underwater elements were shot in a swimming pool in Shepherd's Bush. The bits showing the band playing the song focus on plenty of individual vigour, notably from the brothers Nelson, with Matthew frantically trying to throw his arms and hands away.

The band managed to play 'Which Way Should I Jump?' three times on BBC 1 in less than three weeks in February 1991. Firstly, live on *Blue Peter* – the first band ever to do so – when Matthew was interviewed by John Leslie. According to Nian: '*That was a fucking laugh. That was one of those things that was, like,* Do we do it or do we not do it? Is it going to be credible in the press? *In the end we just thought, Fuck it, we'll do it if we can play live. And we did and it came off alright.*'

Then miming on *Wogan* on 6 February and finally, too early on Saturday morning, on *Going Live!* as mentioned previously… They managed to get to Nottingham and play a gig at the University the same night too. Says Simon: '*You were asking about gig anecdotes the other day. One, not necessarily funny but demonstrating just how far we'd actually come, was when we played the Buttery Bar at Nottingham University on the evening of our earlier performance with Phillip Schofield and Sarah Greene on* Going Live! *in mid February 1991 (we had gone Top 40 by then). This had been the venue where Tropical Blue (later to become the*

Word Association) had made some of its first tentative and largely unappreciated appearances. In typical Milltown Brothers fashion, I couldn't fully enjoy the moment as I had laryngitis (no backing vocals that night) ... but quite a journey to arrive back there at such a high point in our career.'

The gig at Nottingham was one of 14 they played in support of 'Which Way Should I Jump?'. The first of these was at the Lion Street Club in Telford on 1 February. On the way to the gig, the band listened to Radio 1's Round Table and heard guest reviewer John Peel deliver his verdict on their single: *'I wouldn't get up to turn that off.'*

It wasn't meant in a good way, in case you were wondering, but the band thought it was hilarious.

The tour closed with the band headlining both nights of a two-night Northern England extravaganza in one of Paris's most evocative venues, L Locomotive in Pigalle, on 22 and 23 February. Simon, undoubtedly a lover of redemption, has fond memories of these gigs too, referencing the cramped year he spent shacked up with the other two members of the Word Association in his tiny student place in Paris in 1984/1985.

Within a week the band would be out again in the UK, supporting The La's on a 20-date tour.

As the single after the soft release and before the release of their debut album *Slinky*, to be followed by the single that was going to be the huge breakthrough hit – 'Here I Stand' – it did its job perfectly. *NME*'s single of the week, 'B' listed on Radio 1, No.10 in the *Billboard* alternative rock chart in America, and it spent two weeks in the Top 40 in the UK. Maybe they might have expected a bit more and a *Top of the Pops* appearance, but A&M wanted that later, after the album came out in March.

Alan 'Nobby' Hopkinson

In the best part of two years it took the band to produce four singles, sign to A&M and record their first album, they played live all over the place with increasing frequency and intensity. In

Nobby in Milltown's Burnley shirt

1989 it was 60 gigs; in 1990. a few more than that; and come 1991, the band managed well over a 100, by which time they'd switched booking agents to Nigel Hassler at Primary, a natural progression as the band grew and horizons expanded. They also made 13 radio and TV appearances in an intense nine-month period between October 1990 and July 1991. And along the way they were lucky to meet a brilliant sound engineer and front of house, Alan Hopkinson – or Nobby as he's better known in the music industry.

The band first bumped into Nobby at a Trinity College gig in Cambridge in the summer of 1989. Something fired and touched him about the Milltown Brothers. It was more than them being a good live band, he'd experienced plenty of those. Perhaps it's what Steve Lamacq felt on that early Friday night in the Bull & Gate and what others, including *Time Out*, mentioned: *'Cherubic and evil.'* The balance of light and dark – angelic yet mesmerisingly powerful and confident. It was just quietly there, among a bunch of effervescent engaging boy-men having fun and making great music. Big hearts, boundless enthusiasm. Not saints, but no shit. Nobby instantly got it – *'naïve yet potent'* – thought they were going places and wanted to join in. As he left the Cambridge gig, he nipped into the back of the Milltown Brothers' van and left a calling card, using a thick black Sharpie to scrawl his phone number and a brief message across the plywood liner. *'If you need me call. Nobby xx'*

They did. And from then on, he was with them all the way – from Cambridge to the Crystal Palace Bowl, Reading Festival (three times) to CBGBs in New York, St David's University in Lampeter to King Tut's Wah Wah Hut in Glasgow, all over North America, Europe and eventually Japan. You'll find a full list of all the band's gigs that can be remembered at the back of this book. Remarkably, the original five who played the first gig in Didsbury played the most recent gigs at the 100 Club on Oxford Street, London and the Trades Club in Hebden Bridge, 38 years later – and there've been less than a handful of gigs that any of the band have missed during that time.

Nobby put together what he describes as a seriously feisty crew to support them, including at various times Scotty, Spike, Anorak Man, French Pete, Luton, the Cloak and Andy Proudfoot. And, of course, he's the person outside of the band who's most familiar with Matthew's on-stage catchphrase: *'This is our Favourite song.'*

Anyone who's seen the band play is likely to have heard him utter it quite a few times. The rest of the band think he may have said it over a dozen times in one night. Matthew has tried to stop saying it but failed miserably. The joke has been taken to extremes in recent years online. When any song is mentioned or shared, Matthew – or someone on his behalf – always comments: *'This is our Favourite song',* well over 30 years after issue No.2 of their fanzine *Coming From The Mill* featured this letter from Grant, London SE1.

'I have seen the Milltown Brothers three times in the past few months, the first being in March when they toured with The La's. I think they're a great live band but I have to admit to one small niggle. I wish that Matt would make up his bloody mind as to which song is their favourite and not insist on telling us that every other song is. That joke really is wearing thin.'

Others agreed:

'Before nearly half the songs in the hour-long set, Matt Nelson dryly (sic) but cheekily declared 'This is our favourite song.' Steve Hochman, *LA Times*, 25 July 1991.

'Hiding in the bushes is rapidly becoming more inviting than being told by Matt Nelson that this is our favourite song for the fourth time.' Steve Lamacq, 'Crystal Palace Bowl', *NME*, June 1991.

Nobby was born – and grew up – in the heart of London in Holborn in 1963, played in a band before taking an interest in what was going on at the other end of the venue and borrowed £1500 from his dad when an opportunity to buy into a partnership with a half decent PA materialised. Cue the ridiculously long tail of punk after the initial explosion. Live music boiled over all over the place across London in the early 1980s. The music and bands were raw, full of energy and loud, and Nobby, a physically imposing man with an even bigger personality, learned his trade on the job. He ended up being in-house sound engineer at iconic venues – the 100 Club, Marquee and Astoria – at various times in the '80s. The Astoria had a hard-earned reputation for taking 'difficult' gigs other venues were unwilling to risk. Nobby was part of most of these. When Tad, Mudhoney and Nirvana played there in October 1989, Nobby was on the sound desk... and the Milltown Brother's manager Tim Paton was doing his second job – photographing bands. Nirvana were first on and Kurt Cobain's smashed guitar serendipitously landed at Tim's feet.

After four years with the Milltown Brothers, Nobby has gone on to have long relationships with a number of hugely popular, influential, complex and explosive global bands, including Rage

Against the Machine, System of a Down and Tool, along with artists in the UK as diverse as Bush and Jess Glynne. Now in his early 60s and, depending who you ask, between 6' 5" and 6' 7" tall, he still has the enthusiasm and fire of a 20-year-old. He's fulfilled all his ambitions and worked all the venues, including Wembley and Madison Square Gardens, so suggests now that he's considering winding down. He says this having just completed a 16-date arena tour of Europe with Tool in 2024, playing to audiences of 20,000 plus a night.

The mutual respect and love between him and every member of the Milltown Brothers is palpable even now: talk of having each other's backs and lifelong friends is rife. He even met his wife Lee at a Milltown Brothers gig in 1990; she was known as the Bootleg Girl and was doing the merchandise. Naturally the band attended his wedding and party in the evening at the Marquee (not a marquee, *The* Marquee), when the buffet was laced with something that gave everyone a brilliant night.

Nobby's been all over the world involved with huge gigs, but one he still puts in his Top 10 is the the Milltown Brothers at ULU on October 1990, supported by Flowered Up, the Boogie Brothers and Ocean Colour Scene. It was mental. The 1200-capacity gig was sold out and the touts were fighting each other. Nian recalls being in the backstage toilet. *'I'm stood there having a pee and there's this enormous kerfuffle from the tiny frosted window. Next thing I know, this big lad tumbles through it and on to the floor, don't know how he squeezed through it, and he's covered in scratches and ripped clothes and blood and stuff. He hasn't a clue where he is other than in the building and no idea who I am, but he apologises and says he's desperate to see the band, so I slipped off my all-areas pass, gave it to him and off he went.'*

Nobby is more succinct. *'It was a huge night. One of the very best.'*

Part 3

CLIMAX (1991)

'We had a shit life before this and now this isn't shit.'
Matthew tries lying, *Q*, September 1991

Slinky

By 1991 the Milltown Brothers were moving ever faster along a steep upward curve: their debut album was released a year after they were signed by A&M, on 23 March 1991. It entered the UK album chart at 27 and got a remarkable five stars in *Q* magazine. *'An accolade* Q *at that point would normally only reserve for REM albums,'* said Stuart Maconie on Radio 6 Music, 14 September 2024.

Somewhat strangely it only just crept into *Q*'s Top 50 albums of the year, among a host of four-star pretenders who had somehow usurped it...

But I can't jump straight to the music on the album, because there's one crap thing about it: the name. It couldn't be more inappropriate. It has nothing to do with the Milltown Brothers, them as people, or the huge joyful sound they make. *'The inappropriately titled* Slinky *(a more suitable name would be 'Jaunty') has won reviews that established names might envy. Fresh, spirited and bursting with melodies, it has brought premature comparisons with dizzying names such as REM and The Byrds,'* wrote Alan Jackson in the *Observer*, July 1991.

Was it an attempt to balance the whole Milltown Brothers image? You couldn't get a word further removed from the band name if you tried. It was while the band were on tour with The La's that they discovered it and somehow thought it was a great name. *'The La's were probably responsible for the album title* Slinky,*'*

Nian explains. *'We were with them at the Columbia Hotel, both bands drinking and enjoying the moment. A girl walks through the bar and in a deep scouse drawl under their breath they growl "Slllliiinnkky" and continue to do so when every girl walks by. We took it and I'm guessing we're not proud of that. We'd have preferred something much more personal, more us, but that's where it came from...'*

Yet even though it sounds wrong, if it had been based on that springy toy that could walk downstairs, I'd love it. All the kids whose mum and dad seemed to be able to get them everything (in my admittedly slightly more distant childhood) – e.g. a Chopper bike, a Johnny 7, Ben Sherman shirt – had a Slinky. But its provenance and tone are so far from the earthy, honest, a touch naïve, uplifting romantic stuff that is the Milltown Brothers, it was an act of self-sabotage Rivalled only by the artwork that would appear on their second album.

Although The La's aren't my responsibility, I can only apologise on behalf of all involved. Different times, and they were young and feckless too.

In comparison the graphics – first used on the rerecorded 'Which Way Should I Jump?' single and showing the band members thrashing about in water – were not too bad at all. Come to think of it, *Thrashing About* or *Treading Water* might have made a much better album title.

As to the music, it is very, very good. Arguably great. All the tracks were freshly recorded in Moles Studio, Bath and Lillie Yard Studios, West Brompton, during the summer and autumn of 1990, overseen and mixed by producer Dave Meegan.

'Which Way Should I Jump?' is the oldest song on the album, 'Real' the last to be written. Matthew and Simon were credited with writing 'Apple Green', 'Here I Stand', 'Which Way Should I Jump?' and 'Something Cheap'. It was Matthew alone for 'Sally Ann', 'Nationality', 'Sandman' and 'Real', and the Milltown Brothers for 'Never Come Down Again' and 'Seems To Me'.

'Which Way Should I Jump?' was remixed by Bob Kraushaar, and 'Here I Stand', 'Never Come Down Again' and 'Seems To

Me' by Tony Philips. A&M expected these tracks to get the radio airplay and wished to load them with a little extra. The broader timeline of the songs' origins is as follows:

In June and July 1989 'Which Way Should I Jump?' was demoed at EMI Studios in London and recorded with Chris Allison producing in Strawberry Studios.

In December 1989 'Seems To Me' and 'Something Cheap' were demoed in London for A&M with Chris Allison producing.

Overnight 3–4 April 1990 'Don't Breathe In', 'Apple Green' and 'We're Doing Fine' were demoed in the final session at Strawberry Studios. 'Don't Breathe In' is thought to have been Dave Meegan's favourite Milltown Brothers track of all. It's one of my top three favourites too. Amazingly it wasn't liked by A&M – and Matthew thought it nothing special either – which persuaded the band not to include it on the album. For me it's a quietly wondrous song, with a lovely title. At the very least it should have been on the next album, and never have ended up simply as the B-side of 'Here I Stand'. 'We're Doing Fine' appeared on the album with a new title, 'Never Come Down Again'. An absolute banger, it's in my top three too… it had been some session.

During May a similarly productive session at Loft Studios in Camden delivered demos for three tracks that would appear on the album: 'Here I Stand', 'Nationality' and 'Sally Ann'.

Pre-production meetings going through all the songs with Dave took place in Denton, Manchester in May and June 1990. The band then moved into Moles Studio in Bath for the rest of June, July and the beginning of August. 'Sandman' was demoed and most of the recording for all the tracks took place. It was a blissful time for the band.

At the insistence of A&M – and with the aim of getting the album finished – they reluctantly relocated to Lillie Yard Studios, West Brompton for six weeks from mid-August to early October. They lived in a flat in Ladbroke Grove in Notting Hill, with Seal in the flat next door while recording his eponymously titled debut album. Endless mixes of 'Killer' and 'Crazy' serenaded them throughout their stay.

The band headed out on a 22-date headline tour of the UK in October, having been expected to complete the album by then. The tour ended somewhat conveniently with shows at the Moles Club in Bath and the Fleece and Firkin in Bristol. The band – poor things – complained so much about leaving Bath and being kept awake by Seal that A&M allowed them to go back to Moles Studio in November to finish the album.

It was now that 'Real' and the final version of 'Never Come Down Again' – both essentially studio-developed and quite rampantly joyous tracks – were recorded. Final mixing took place at Maison Rouge in Fulham and the album was deemed complete on 19 December 1990.

The band to a man were extremely happy with it, and still are. Only Barney was miffed at how low the keyboards had been mixed. But as a unit they felt it was as good a statement as they could have made about what they were capable of, outside of their best live performances.

They ended up releasing four singles from the album. Yet to my ears at least, there are two, maybe three or four more songs on *Slinky* which in many other band's canon would have been high on the list of likely single material.

The band that always wanted to make albums appear to have delivered the best of both worlds with a debut album full of potential hit singles. The only two songs that for me aren't single material – and I wouldn't have on the album – are 'Nationality' and 'Sandman'. *'Mind you the awful stadium thud of 'Nationality' should have been binned under Simple Minds outtakes'* wrote Dave Simpson in *Melody Maker*, March 1991. *'Side one's closing track 'Nationality' is horribly close to those old Irish windbags U2, bloated as it is…'* noted Paul Moody for *Sounds*, March 1991.

Other than demonstrating variety and scope, I don't get how they made the final cut. Replace them with 'Don't Breathe In' and 'When It Comes', and it could have been as close to perfect a debut as it's possible to get. All 10 songs on the album could have been considered as possible singles. How many bands have more than a handful of songs – never mind 10 – really worthy of consideration as singles in an entire career, never mind hanging around their first album? And then they went and called it *Slinky*.

Slinky spent five weeks in the UK album chart but got no higher than 27 in its first week of release and sold over 100,000 worldwide. On the face of it a brilliant start, sufficiently good for A&M to take up the contractual option of a second album. And I'm sure when they started out the band would have been delighted to know they'd rack up a Top 30 album within three years or so. And then get the chance to make another. With appearances in both *NME*'s and *Q*'s Top 50 albums of the year, outstanding reviews and crossover potential. Here was a band getting great exposure both on the road and across media. Ambitions grew; they were doing it.

And this book hasn't yet finished with the eulogies to *Slinky*.

'Here I Stand'

Hot on the heels of *Slinky* came the release of the Milltown Brothers' fifth single, 'Here I Stand', on 13 April 1991. It has quite wonderful cover art. Whatever visual and naming aberrations occurred elsewhere in the band's career, this more than makes up for it. Put it side by side with the cover of second album *Valve*. How could this be from the same band?

'Here I Stand'

Here I stand
Ponytail and flares
Waiting your command
Here I stand.

And here I fall
Watched by one and all,
To the flies on the wall
Here I fall.

Round and round and round again
Around again we go
Never stop to think or say hello.

Here I stand
Both feet in the sand
Sinking as I am
Here I stand.

And here I stay
Forever and a day
With countless counting people
Counting time.

Round and round and round we go
Around again once more
Never stop to think just who we are.

Here I stand
Putty in your hand
Gathered in command
Here I stand.

Round and round and round we go
Around again too slow
Never get to where we want to go

Lead me on.
Here I Stand.
Lead me on.
Here I Stand.

It was released on 7" vinyl, backed by 'Don't Breathe In'; CD and 12" purple vinyl had one additional track 'Jack Lemmon'; and the regular 12" vinyl all these plus 'Something On My Mind'. The title track was credited to Matthew and Simon, 'Don't

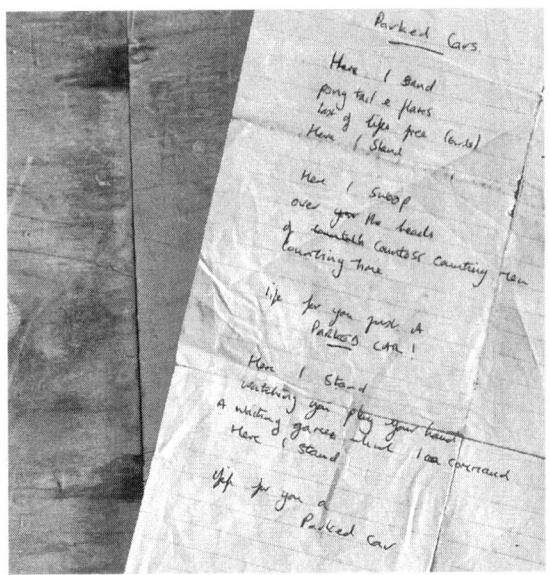

Parked Cars handwritten lyrics

Breathe In' to Matthew alone, and the other two to the Milltown Brothers. 'Here I Stand' had been held back for quite some time, having begun life as a song called 'Parked Cars', and in its final version was the song that would break the band significantly in the UK, its crossover mainstream potential obvious.

'A'-listed on Radio 1 for three weeks, ever-improving singles sales for every previous release, a song with a big happy yet yearning hook and melody, and a midweek industry forecast already in the Top 30 – a Top 20 chart entry in the first week looked likely and an appearance on *Top of the Pops* pencilled in. Expectation was an understatement.

The only slightly disappointing thing about the single was the video released alongside it, completely devoid as it was of... well anything much, other than the most literal interpretation of the song lyrics imaginable. The director who made it said he wanted to make an expensive video that looked like it cost nothing. He certainly delivered on the latter.

The band play the song on Wandsworth Common in a completely loose and disinterested way, half the time just standing around, looking at traffic. Get it? Rather than being interspersed with the band doing anything vaguely interesting, it's a few clips of the band doing distinctly average and cheesy things, in camera or manipulated on film. Rising up like dominoes fall... to... 'stand'. The camera doing a 360 on '*Round and round and round again*'. All in a strange pinky-purple tint.

Perhaps the most engaging thing on the video is Barney wearing a lemon shirt walking behind everyone, closely followed by Matthew doing his shaking his hands off thing, and a couple of dogs and a cyclist cutting through the frame. And then they all walk off in black and white against an orange sky, disappearing into a rapidly diminishing black-framed circle.

Distinctly average but no worries, they were going to be on *Top of the Pops*. The video was dismissed as unfortunate but irrelevant, it would hardly be seen, they'd be playing it live all over the TV.

What else? Idiosyncratic as it may seem, A&M saw fit to release 'Here I Stand' on a double A-side promotional 12" single in Brazil with a song that had been No.1 10 years earlier, 'Tainted Love' by Soft Cell, on the other side. Nobody seems to know why.

And a couple of years later the song's crossover appeal was underlined when it was chosen as the theme music for *All Quiet on the Preston Front*, a comedy drama series that took place in the fictional Lancashire town of Roker Bridge, and part of which was filmed in Church Street in Padiham, within a mile of where Barney had been brought up. It won a number of awards for best comedy drama and gave the band a fresh opportunity to appear on TV... The great final flourish for a big hit?

12 Hours

10 July 1991, 7 p.m. It began with a rapturous reception on the band's second appearance on *Wogan*, prime time BBC 1.

They mimed their way through the remixed and rereleased single 'Apple Green' – the follow-up to 'Here I Stand'.

> *"Play your hearts out, lads" beams Terry Wogan, as Milltown Brothers glumly file past him… Afterwards, everyone is smiles and the verdict is that the Milltown Brothers have never looked better on television… "Do you know" says guitarist Simon Nelson, ginger haired and affable, "I used to sit and watch bands on The Tube and think, Fucking hell, I'd cut my right arm off to do that and how do you do it anyway?" Q,* September 1991.

Ginger haired. I'm smiling. Two hours later they played a sold-out gig at one of London's most iconic venues, the 2000-capacity Astoria in Soho, with Nobby on familiar territory.

Then they enjoyed a few mad hours in the Columbia, the legendary rock 'n' roll roll hotel on Hyde Park, before catching an early morning flight on 11 July to New York for their first US tour. *'Last night it was Wogan and the Astoria. Tomorrow the world?'* asked Max Bell in the *Evening Standard*, 11 July 1991.

Says Barney, *'It just felt surreal, getting cars everywhere, partying with all manner of people we'd previously only seen on the TV, and I'm there thinking, This is crazy, how the hell has all this happened?'*

Says Matthew, *'A couple of things happened that could have derailed all this and somehow they were magically resolved. First I was stopped in Hyde Park smoking a joint by the police outside the Columbia and then that night I realised I'd no idea where my passport was and got on the flight to America the next morning without it, which you could back then, the checking being done in the States. The police let me off with a caution for the joint and as I was walking through JFK this guy materialised from somewhere and gave me my passport. You have to laugh.'*

The band had only just finished yet another tour, 20 dates in Europe in June, featuring one show in the UK: a huge gig at the Crystal Palace Bowl headlined by the Pixies, whose Black Francis dropped by to tell them how much he loved 'Which Way Should

I Jump?'. The half-dozen gigs they played in America included headline shows at Whisky a Go Go in Hollywood and CBGBs in New York. During the tour the band stayed for a couple of nights at another legendary rock 'n' roll hotel, the Hyatt on Sunset Strip. In the late 1980s and '90s a true rock 'n' roll great, Little Richard, had taken up residence there. After a long afternoon in the bar, the band found his suite of rooms and politely knocked on the door. His son answered: Little Richard wasn't receiving guests. The Milltown Brothers went away and returned. Four times. On the fifth occasion Little Richard answered. Full make-up, towering black pompadour and glittering stage outfit. He gave them the once-over – '*Ooooo, my soul. Hello, boys.*' – and proceeded to hold court for a few minutes. The band chatted gibberish, Little Richard whooped and hollered a bit and gave them each a religious text, *Finding Peace Within* by Mrs E.G. White, as the audience drew to a close.

Nirvana

At the time this gig seemed only a little out of the ordinary. Monday, 23 September 1991, the Milltown Brothers' sixth date on their second American tour of 1991 in Boston. A small festival of 11 bands playing in a few bars, all in the same street. Alternative radio station WNFX's 8th birthday party. They played with equal billing alongside Nirvana, the Wonder Stuff – being supported by the Milltown Brothers on the tour – and the Smashing Pumpkins among others.

The gig was later described by the *Boston Phoenix* as the second biggest gig in the city's history – after James Brown's 5 April 1968 show at the Boston Garden, which took place the day after Martin Luther King was assassinated. Then, urban America was up in arms, protest and riots swept across the country, and the show was almost cancelled, but the authorities turned it on its head and insisted it be televised live in the Boston area. Everyone wanted to watch it, the rioting was minimised, and the city was saved from the worst of the trouble.

For the Milltown Brothers, the competition was intimidating, but the band agree they played one of their best gigs ever, despite Matthew having a filthy cold and being out of his head on cough medicine. They did their level best to steal the show and thought they might have done, the crowd had been with them. Then they went next door to see the band that people were talking about, who were releasing their second album the next day. They witnessed Nirvana being announced on stage in front of a frenzied crowd of 1000: *'Would you please welcome the fucking coolest band in the world.'* They weren't sure about what they were hearing, any melody in the songs impossible to discern in the wail of brutalised instruments and the live chaos that ensued.

Says Simon now, *'I was at the back but just remember the crowd bouncing all over the place and their sweat violently raining back down on them from this low ceiling, I'd never heard of them.'*

Barney remembers, *'I walked in on this heavy thrashing thing, having been told I had to go and see this band that were on next door. Kurt was just throwing himself into the crowd and screaming. I didn't get it at all but the people who were in there, you couldn't help but feel something was going on.'*

A few days after the festival the Milltown Brothers got a brilliant note from the promoter. It wasn't just the band who thought they'd delivered.

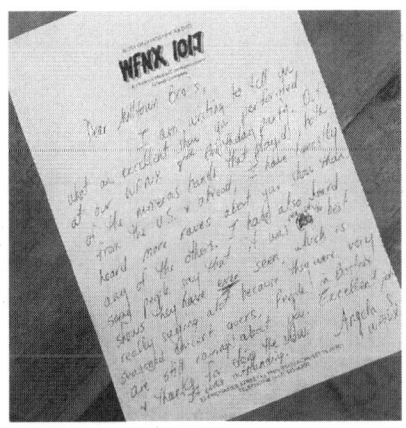

Part 4
FALLING (1991–1994)

'This is very dark with some hallelujah shards of a watery luminescence, most of which never saw the light of day.'
Simon

Peripeteia

Peripeteia is a word of Greek origin with a lovely sound belying its meaning: *'a turning point or sudden reversal of fortune or change in circumstances.'* Ridiculously apt for the Milltown Brothers (and Icarus in more extreme and tragic circumstances).

While the band were having enormous fun in America, first by themselves, then on their one-night stand with Nirvana – to be repeated 11 months later at Reading Festival in 1992, when things had changed massively for both bands – and on their more extensive experience with the Wonder Stuff; and while they were looking forward to their first tour of Japan in February 1992; and while they were demoing what they thought were promising new songs here, there and everywhere, their parabola insidiously experienced an easing off from the steep upward trajectory to what proved to be a plateau – from where the only way to go for parabolas is down.

This was compounded by a bunch of increasingly terrible decisions made by the band, difficult to understand happenings or non-happenings at A&M, and unfathomable absences of band or band activity in the right places at the right time. They were maybe a little too confident and expectant, unused to things going wrong and unfamiliar with the associated novelty of pressure, too naïve, easy-going and muddle-headed by what was going on.

It all started after the release of 'Here I Stand' in April 1991.

Absolutely Robbed

The astonishing failure of 'Here I Stand' to break into the Top 40 in April 1991 was the first and most significant blow. If there was one turning point, this was it. Even as the band sold out the Astoria, appeared on *Wogan*, toured America twice, attended the 1991 *Q* Awards as one of the year's most exciting newcomers who'd *'cracked it'* in 1991 and had fun in Japan in February 1992, they'd already suffered a setback that they got no chance to put right – and which proved directly or indirectly responsible for more or less everything else that unfolded.

As to how this happened, let's jump forward to start the story in the right place. The Q Awards in 1991 were held at Abbey Road Studios. Simon, Matthew and Barney rocked up to find themselves on the same table as their record label stablemates Del Amitri. At the time their lead singer, Justin Currie, sported a pair of the most magnificent sideburns to be seen this side of Elvis's *'68 Comeback Special*. Barney now recreated – in slightly less offence-causing circumstances – his Town & Country REM moment and brought the house that was the table down by asking if Justin had a roadie dedicated to caring for the sideburns in question... All of this was happening a short while before the December 1991 issue of *Vox* hit the streets with an unexplained sentence referencing the Milltown Brothers and 'Here I Stand' by respected Radio 1 DJ, keeper of *The Evening Session* and guardian of the Top 40 chart at the time, Mark Goodier.

'They're really good and have been absolutely robbed of a chart hit.'

A year or so earlier he'd made a point of predicting the band's future success in *Rage* magazine (November 1990), having just had the second of two sessions with them when they played 'Which Way Should I Jump?', 'When It Comes', 'Here I Stand' and 'Sally Ann', a session broadcast on Radio 1, on 3 December 1990. *'And the future? Watch out for these names. The Milltown Brothers, Ocean Colour Scene, Blur and Paris Angels. Better still listen out for them on my show.'*

And it was during Mark's stewardship of the chart count-down that 'Here I Stand' was expected to break into the Top 30 after its release on 13 April 1991. The band had even agreed they'd appear on *Top of the Pops* the following week – as A&M had planned – which would instantly give them and 'Here I Stand' massive exposure, guaranteeing many more sales and just as significantly, provide a big boost for *Slinky*, which had arrived in the album chart at a lofty 27 a couple of weeks earlier. Anything was possible. Having been told they were already in the Top 30 midweek, the band remember listening to the countdown and getting increasingly excited as the song wasn't mentioned and the count reached No.30. They were in the Top 30!

By the time it reached 20 and 'Here I Stand' still hadn't been mentioned, wild expectation and anticipation – surely they hadn't gone Top 20 – was starting to be replaced by nagging concern. They soon discovered 'Here I Stand' wasn't in the Top 40 at all.

The story broke shortly after. In unusual if not unprece-dented circumstances, Gallup, who managed the chart, decided at the last minute that too many of the sales of 'Here I Stand' had taken place in the north of England and simply reduced the northern sales across the board to make the figure more repre-sentative of sales throughout the UK.

It appears there were three independent local record shops in Burnley, Preston and Accrington, where the band had made last-minute personal appearances to boost already high sales on their home patch. These were identified as having suspiciously high sales, such that Gallup felt it necessary to adjust the band's total sales right across the north of the country. But as an exam-ple, HMV shops in the major northern cities – who hadn't had any band appearances at all – were showing very healthy sales too. So why should they and everywhere else in the north – how-ever that was defined – have been included in the adjustment?

It's difficult to find any single that was so high profile and expected to chart being similarly treated in such a broad-brush way. After all, it had been 'A' listed for three weeks on Radio 1 before its release date, and there must have been many, many instances of an inordinate number of sales of singles around London, Liverpool, Glasgow and other major cities throughout the history of the chart, when a band from the area catches fire.

It left 'Here I Stand' to enter the chart at No.48, miserable given what 'Which Way Should I Jump?' had achieved and given too that it was at 35 in the mid-week figures given to the band. As all three of the in-store appearances identified by Gallup took place after these figures were issued, the level of weighting was a grotesque overreaction at best. It lost the guaranteed chart position it had earned before they took place, a large proportion of its first week sales, all momentum and – crucially – the *Top of the Pops* appearance that had been agreed.

The dawning reality of it being a punitive, life-changing penalty rather than the 'weighting' it was euphemistically described as would be realised over the coming months and years. Because, for all manner of reasons, they would never get the chance to right the wrong, not least because their luck ran out. Yet still 'Here I Stand' was able to sell enough in the following weeks to climb tantalisingly to within one spot – 41 – of what would have triggered a *Top of the Pops* appearance. But maybe that was never going to happen once the headline had emerged publicly and the single was associated with it.

Mark Goodier's unsolicited but presumably well-informed and honest comment suggests the single had been well and truly hung out to dry, so much so that A&M petitioned, then briefly considered suing Gallup for their intervention. An article raising questions appeared in *NME*, yet while the decision was disappointing and with hindsight the most overt, critical and damaging reverse the band received, causing repercussions all over the place, the band were remarkably sanguine. They thought they'd sort it with the next song.

Nian told *Coming From The Mill* in 1991, *'It was weighted out of the chart by Gallup because we sold a lot in the north – well, loads in the north and around Leeds, Liverpool and Manchester. It went in at 35 originally and Gallup thought it wasn't fair that we had so many sales up north and it wasn't centred over the whole country. They weighted us back to 48 and after that it was really hard to get it back up. We'd sold a lot in the first week and those sales were effectively lost and over the next few weeks we could only get it up to number 41. It's not important, though it pissed us off at the time, but that's not what we're into, singles.'*

This frighteningly relaxed attitude demonstrated both an easy confidence they could just do it with the next single, and a lack of awareness of the impact of what had happened. While it may not have been important to them from the point of view of the success of the single – hey, who are they kidding? – it was crucial for A&M that they had hit singles to recoup their investment in the band. More important still, the failure had a profound impact on the level of exposure and therefore the commercial success of what was a rather more than good first album – with an unappealing and unrepresentative title. They'd not established themselves with a wider audience and were about to disappear to America and Japan for eight months and they needed the hit – a good foothold – to remain front of mind with the music-buying public. *Top of the Pops* would definitively have provided that and justified and stimulated more single releases.

As it was, *Slinky* peaked at 27 in its first week of release and, despite all the glowing reviews in the music press, disappeared. The 100,000 copies eventually sold weren't enough to pay for it, and although the band and A&M viewed the album as a big success it quietly did significantly less well than either it should have or deserved to do – and, indeed, would have done in the normal course of events.

As to further evidence of the abiding quality of *Slinky*, here's a completely chance conversation on Radio 6 Music overheard 33 years later as I was writing this chapter:

Sean (a caller to the programme): '*... we go from the Alessi Brothers to the Milltown Brothers and 'Here I Stand' and it's a fabulously jaunty song for a Saturday morning... strangely I only picked up the record* Slinky, *the album, about a month ago from Vinyl Planet in Macclesfield... the first side of that album is probably the* *best A-side of an album – certainly in the top 5 – I've ever listened to, there's some marvellous songs on it, and it's not usually my kind of bag...'*

Stuart Maconie (after playing 'Here I Stand' on *Radcliffe and Maconie*, Radio 6 Music, 14 September 2024) said: *'Sean is not alone in his enthusiasm for that album* Slinky, *it got five stars in* Q *magazine... and a lot of the reviews saying what a classic album that is.'*

No New Singles

Disappointingly the only response from A&M to the controversial failure of 'Here I Stand' was a prosaic decision to reissue a 'harder-hitting' remixed version of 'Apple Green' as the follow-up on 6 July 1991, even though it had been released the first time around only eight months earlier in October 1990, when it got to 82 in the chart. The 7" vinyl was backed with 'We've Got Time', the CD and 12" vinyl also had 'So You Want To Be A Writer' and the lovely 'Drop Like A Stone', and a special 12" EP featured completely different additional tracks, an acoustic version of 'Sally Ann' and demos of 'Nationality' and 'Something Cheap'.

It came with a 'harder-hitting' new video too, but beneath its ebullient tone it simply continued the well-trodden theme of the band playing the song – in black and white, and rather energetically in this instance – cut with a bewildering library of random, vaguely ethical, eco-related stuff. Trees falling, crop spraying, a green room with a green clad woman and child cutting a green apple, and the band as various characters emphasising their greenness –innocence? – or redness – malevolence? – both of which appear to be harmful to the environment, if you can mentally bridge the gaps between the imagery.

The band have little memory of the making of the video, although there was a significant amount of dramatic dressing up and staging of individual band members to represent a series of stereotypes. Matthew, some kind of underworld boss – if not the devil himself – with slicked-back locks, shades, red shirt and black three-piece suit, sporting a large medallion, sat on a brightly lit, vividly red throne. Nian, a preppy high school geek on a date, confusingly if cutely dualistic in a red silk shirt and green bow tie. Barney and Simon, a couple of 'Pringled' golfers with a red apple as a golf ball being putted across an artificial green into the hole. James, a vaguely pagan and somewhat pale and interesting Adam in the garden pondering a red apple, presumably immediately prior to his expulsion. A complex and surreal mash of scenarios and ideas which could easily be interpreted as a wonderfully ornate and elaborate representation of Matthew's stream of consciousness…

Despite being a rerelease and without the build-up, level of Radio 1 support and exposure both 'Which Way Should I Jump?' and 'Here I Stand' received, it still managed to get to 43 in the charts. Which suggests 'Here I Stand' had been a certainty to enter the Top 40. So why didn't A&M choose to release a completely new single instead of 'Apple Green'? Or follow it up with a new single? It can't possibly have been because they didn't think they had songs of the right quality. 'Never Come Down Again', 'Real' or 'Sally Ann' could easily have provided the fresh impetus to get the band in the Top 40 and on *Top of the Pops*. So, apart from crass stupidity, neglect or a cooling of interest within the label, what are the reasons that could possibly explain why A&M chose neither option? The answer seems to come down to cost – which at this stage and within the context of the relationship was neither here nor there, they'd already invested so much in the band. Or, it could be that four songs from the album had already been released as singles and A&M now believed that a fifth was going to the well once too often – even if three of them had been issued long before *Slinky* was released and they'd never had a bona fide Top 30 hit with any of them.

It's difficult to understand the thinking: the absence of activity is incredible, especially given that the band already had new music available, including 'Falling Straight Down' and the revised version of 'When It Comes', among a bunch of other non-*Slinky* songs, both of which would eventually be considered good enough to be lead tracks on their second album.

This was a band with momentum, who'd almost managed a bona fide hit with a rereleased song, writing great songs and hammering on the door, who after their second appearance on *Wogan* had gone on to play a sold-out headline gig at the Astoria the same evening, then flown off for their first American tour early the next day, riding the crest of a wave and due to headline some of the most iconic US venues – is it possible to believe that this band would not release another single until almost two years later, in May 1993?

Disappeared

On arrival in America, the band almost immediately had technical issues with hastily prepared hired gear at two of the shows at the Danceteria and CBGBs in New York. The most serious of these was at CBGBs, where the bass amp blew up. This needlessly soured the rest of their visit because both shows were heavily attended by American A&M personnel and lots of *'important and influential'* people in the American music industry and A&M interpreted this as the band lacking professionalism. Coupled with the failure of 'Here I Stand', it convinced them that the band weren't ready for a full headline tour of the country, which had been the plan.

Yet none of this darkened in any shape or form the positive reviews of their performances – quite the opposite. For Kerry Faustmann at the CBGB's gig, the bass amp blowing up was a masterstroke. *'The highlight of the show for me was when something happened with James' bass amp and the band had to wait while it was being repaired, but Matt and Simon didn't want to wait and so they kept the audience entertained with folk songs. It was an incredible spur-of-the-moment thing that showed another side of their talent... the show was incredible, it was the most amazing night of my life.'*

Unwisely, the band was undeterred: they were too eager to

enjoy more of America and with the support and insistence of Harold Berman, head of A&M in the UK, they went back there in September by accepting an invitation to support the Wonder Stuff on their tour. They'd returned to Europe for just three shows – the 1991 Reading Festival, the Nijmijen gig supporting Simple Minds and a sold-out headline show at De Doelen in Rotterdam. But much as they love the Wonder Stuff, it wasn't their tour and not their audience and the Wonder Stuff had no real pretentions or desire to break America, while the Milltown Brothers thought they could and wanted to be there. Delightfully for the Wonder Stuff, but rather cruelly for the Milltown Brothers given the 'Here I Stand' debacle, they hit No.1 in the UK with 'Dizzy' while they were in America and were flown back by Concorde in the middle of the tour to do *Top of the Pops*.

What no one appeared to consider was what doing the 27-date American tour meant: after being one of the busiest gigging bands in the UK, repeatedly visible all over the place at a grassroots level throughout 1989 and 1990 and in to the middle of May 1991, the Milltown Brothers effectively disappeared without trace – or a big enough hit, exacerbating and probably prompting the lack of any further single releases.

They went from 200 gigs in three years or so prior to the sold-out Astoria gig in July 1991, with ever bigger audiences and venues, at an increasingly intense rate throughout the UK – including 47 gigs between February and May 1991, one gig in Paris, three BBC TV appearances, two radio sessions and a 20-date European tour in June …

… to just 17 shows in the UK in the year after the Astoria show. The 1991 Reading Festival, ten supporting the Charlatans in April 1992 and six headline shows, all at venues with less than half the capacity of the Astoria.

No new music for over two years – 'Apple Green' having been a rerelease – in a business that is fast-moving and ephemeral at best, where interest disappears quickly and the press – with good reason – is notoriously on the lookout for the next new thing. Quite what anyone connected with the band was thinking to allow this to happen is difficult to understand. Perhaps the acid test of band management is being able to step back when things are going wrong, see the big picture, be abrasive if necessary and take what may be unwelcome action. No such luck.

It's true the band had never felt that close to A&M's people, but given the significant investment in them and the label's decision to take up the option of the second album based on the performance of *Slinky*, it's jaw-dropping that there was no new music, no gigs, no visibility and no news, especially when what would prove to be the one hugely significant and legendary gig of their second tour of America with the Wonder Stuff – and the final highlight of the band's hot summer of 1991 – ended up casting a further shadow over their future.

Bollocks With Pop

As already described, the Milltown Brothers played one of their best gigs alongside Nirvana in Boston on 23 September 1991. The problem was that the next day Nirvana released their second album, *Nevermind*, which eventually changed the dynamic and perception of the gig as a coming of age for Nirvana.

Their first album, *Bleach*, had been released in 1989 to some critical acclaim but only modest sales – 40,000 in America. *Nevermind* itself received limited interest and only a few reviews initially, which were mixed.

But tellingly in the UK that excellent judge Steve Lamacq(!) gave an indication that something was going on by giving *Nevermind* a 9 out of 10 review in *NME*. *'Nirvana do here what Sonic Youth did so emphatically with Goo last year – making the move from cult indie to major label with not as much as a hiccup. In fact, just as the Sonics impressed and outstripped the sceptics' expectations, Nirvana have made an LP which is not only better than anything they've done before, it'll stand up as a new reference point for the future post-hardcore generation... While various American grunge bands seem content to slosh around in their respective hardcore genres – albeit with some success and lucidity – Nirvana have opted out of the underground without wimping out of the creative process. Nevermind is the big American alternative record of the autumn. But better still, it'll last well into next year.'*

Nevermind may well have had an unremarkable arrival, but by Christmas it had gone gold in America, and then platinum, and went on to sell 30 million copies worldwide. Following the Stone Roses' eponymous debut, it was the second paradigm-changing pop/rock album released during the Milltown Brothers' ascent, and its significance swamped that of the Stone Roses. *Nevermind* became one of the most acclaimed and influential albums of all time with a sound Kurt Cobain described as *'The Knack and Bay City Rollers getting molested by Black Flag and Black Sabbath'.*

It brought a seismic shift to the pop/rock musical landscape, such that one moment the Milltown Brothers were close to the centre of what was happening with their pop with bollocks – and the next they were pushed aside by Nirvana's inversion of the equation, what you might call bollocks with pop.

This threw the music industry into a bit of a panic: record companies looked at their roster and wondered where their own Nirvana was. Which was okay for established acts who could go about doing their own thing with their own fans and the mainstream, but for bands like the Milltown Brothers – who by the time of the release of their second album would have had over a million pounds invested in them by A&M, without breaking into the mainstream – it wasn't so straightforward.

To make matters worse, there were rumours of wholesale personnel changes at A&M and the band increasingly felt pushed around and a bit of a problem for the label. Rather than being allowed to develop naturally and do what they'd already proved to be good at – ploughing their own furrow – they were being asked to deliver another *Slinky* and at the same time write songs that responded to the landscape shaped by *Nevermind.* This messed with their heads.

Rejection

The result – propagated and defined by A&M's lack of clarity and negativity – was frantic but fruitless – according to A&M at least. They continued writing and demoing in a variety of places, from pleasant retreats to progressively more modest residential studios as investment in the band began to taper. Nian explains, '*Rose Castle Cottage in Tarn Haws in the Lake District was a beautiful isolated place I'd holidayed in with my mum, dad and brother, we even went there for a few days. I think it's where "Pictures" was written, which I still think is a great song, but A&M weren't having it and were really pushing us to try to do a bunch of things with the songwriting, another "Which Way Should I Jump" and* Nevermind *being the typical starting points. But when you're in a band and writing and it's going well, you're just where you are, creating songs that represent where all your heads are at that moment in time, which reflects everything that's gone before and what's going on there and then, so we just ended up fighting ourselves musically and culturally. We should have stuck to our guns and just did what we wanted and felt right for us... what's the worst that could have happened? We'd have made a record somewhere else on our terms, but we felt we owed them and weren't tough or loud enough.*'

A stack of songs demoed through to the end of 1992, some of which were and are extremely good – and all but one ('Turn Off') were rejected by A&M. Ridiculous doesn't come close. Worse still, no one in or around the band was able or willing to take a stand.

And all the while – for very good reason – the band firmly believed they could have had a second album out at worst by the summer of 1992 with the right support from A&M and the right production team, which would have been at least as good if not significantly better – not least in terms of timing – than the second album that finally came out in an atmosphere of haste, desperation and contractual obligation over a year later.

Not that *Valve* is anywhere near as mediocre as the band has come to believe.

In the early stages of this build-up of tension and frustration, there was at least a brief shaft of '*watery luminescence*' in late February 1992. But it was only ever going to be more of a holiday than a game changer.

Japan

The band independently describe the tour of Japan as the last of the very best of times. And even then it was marred by a horrible tragedy 5000 miles away in Germany.

Michael 'Spike' Hall, a regular member of the crew, didn't make the trip to Japan. He was working for another band in Germany, and was killed in an accident driving their van. It hit the band and Nobby hard. Powerless to do anything about it, they did what they could when they got back from Japan, quickly arranging a benefit gig at Leicester University on 19 March for his family, where the Wonder Stuff big-heartedly supported them, with Nobby front of house. And when they eventually released their second album, 30 months later, it was dedicated to his memory.

A&M's planning for Japan included the Japan-only release of a compilation album, *More Slinky*, in October 1991 and three months later the Japan and European (not UK) release of 'Sally Ann' as a single, backed with an acoustic version of the same song and an early demo of 'Something Cheap'.

More Slinky is a lovely and generous album of older tracks and leftovers from the first album, compiled to give the Japanese something fresh to buy. It has an impressive and long track listing, comprising 'Apple Green' (single remix), 'When It Comes' (which would also appear on *Valve* in a rather different form), 'My Favourite Place', 'Jack Lemmon', 'Natural', 'Knives and Forks', 'Drop Out', 'Diplomat', 'Something Cheap' (demo), 'Don't Breathe In', 'We've Got Time', 'Something On My Mind', 'Silver Town', 'Drop Like A Stone' and 'So You Want To Be A Writer'.

'Sally Ann' is noteworthy for being yet another single released from *Slinky* and brought the surprise return of the green and red umbrella theme – originally used for the first release of 'Apple Green' – for no apparent reason other than it worked quite nicely with the typography of the track listing as part of the CD disc design.

But why weren't the album and single released in the UK market too? Perhaps at a similar time or when it became obvious that the second album was unlikely to appear for ages and neither were any new singles.

The release of *More Slinky* – somehow a much more authentic and appealing title than plain *Slinky* – demonstrated that the Milltown Brothers consistently undervalued and underutilised some at least very good material – starting right back with their first independent single 'Coming From The Mill'. The album includes excellent B-sides and bonus tracks on various single formats, and has a number of songs that might have justifiably been considered as strong new album tracks or, in one or two instances, even singles in their own right. The band and A&M might realistically have considered releasing a completely new and legitimate second album almost immediately, based on what was on *More Slinky* plus songs they already had in the studio and had played live. These included 'Falling Straight Down', 'Turn Me Over', 'Trees', 'Worldwide' and 'Rosemary Page', the first three of which eventually appeared on *Valve* anyway – and the other two probably should have.

But they had always brutally pursued – at Matthew's insistence – a high standard of B-sides and additional single tracks and refused to look back on even recent past work as worth revisiting, reworking or reusing, convinced of their ability to always do better. This didn't serve them well in relation to A&M's low opinion of the band's post *Slinky* demos.

As it is, they were amazed and delighted to find they were recognised in Japan – and that meant a certain amount of colourful personal devotion. Something they'd already experienced with a small number of UK-based Japanese students who followed the band in 1990 and '91. It was an intense week with five sold-out shows at the Shinsaibashi Club Quattro in Osaka, the Nagoya Club Quattro in Nagoya and three consecutive nights at the Shibiya Club Quattro in Tokyo, all with a capacity of 550. There were a huge amount of press and personal appearances squeezed into a week, the highlight being a VIP evening at the Lexington Queen in Tokyo partying with A&M stablemate Bryan Adams, who was globally riding very high with '(Everything I Do), I Do It for You'.

But all too soon they were back to reality, Spike's benefit gig and the short tour supporting the Charlatans.

Innocents

Songs that could have ended up – and the 12 that did – on the Milltown Brothers' second album began to appear as far back as May 1990 and Square One Studio in Bury, where a rather nice song called 'Inkwell' was demoed and recorded. It originally appeared that year on *Home*, a compilation album, alongside songs from Mark E Smith and Paris Angels among others, and eventually turned up on the band's 15-track bonus CD with *Rubberband* in 2004 and 2022 compilation *Tongue-Tied Mesmerised*.

It's worth listing the demos that followed:

July 1990 Loft Studios, Camden: 'When It Comes', 'My Favourite Place', 'Jack Lemmon'

December 1990 DNA Home Studio, Bath: 'Diplomat', 'Knives and Forks', 'World of Opportunity', 'Drop Out'

December 1990 Moles Studio, Bath: 'Don't Breathe In'

April 1991 Barkerhouse Road, Nelson: 'Falling Straight Down', 'Crawl With Me', 'Spring Fever', 'Can't Find the Time', 'The Orange Tree', 'I'm On A Losing Track'

June 1991 Out Of The Blue Studio, Ancoats: 'So You Want To Be A Writer', 'Turn Me Over', 'Drop Like A Stone', 'Different Kind Of Life', 'Got This Feeling', 'Rosemary Page'

November 1991 Jamar Studios, Wokingham: 'Trees', 'Worldwide', 'Merry England', 'Free Feeling', 'Great Adventure', 'That's The Way', 'Lovebite', 'Focus'

January 1992 Chipping Norton Studios: 'Us', 'Trees', 'Falling Straight Down', 'Worldwide'

February 1992 iFortex 4-track, Barrowford: 'Disappear', 'Awaken Your Mind', 'Flowers', '32 Hour Drive'

April 1992 Morecambe: 'Cool Breeze', 'Killing All The Good Men, Jimmy', Changeling, 'Sleepwalking', 'Mind's Eye', 'Long Time'

May 1992 Moles Studio, Bath: 'Crawl With Me', 'Sleepwalking', 'Pictures (Round My Room)'

August 1992 Handley Studios, Burnley: 'Rainbow Woods', 'Turn Off', 'You Don't Know Me No More'

September 1992 Loft Studios, Camden: 'Sweet Nothing'

September 1992 Shamrock Studios, Balderstone: 'Caroline', 'Someday', 'Alice', 'Have We Met Before', 'Older Now'

September 1992 Fortex 4-track, Barrowford: 'The Way I'm Going', 'Please Don't Fall', 'Shelter', 'Put Your Lips Together'

October 1992 Konk Studios, London: 'Turn Off'

December 1992, London: 'It's All Over Now, Baby Blue', 'Everybody Knows'

It's a remarkable output, so what was the reaction?

'All of 1992, A&M didn't rate anything we did apart from "Turn Off". It got to the point where Harold Berman, who was obsessed with "Which Way Should I Jump?" and the whole "pop with bollocks" and West Coast Byrds thing, more or less held us to ransom by forcefully suggesting we covered "It's All Over Now, Baby Blue" as the follow-up single to "Turn Off" and then insisted it went on the second album…

> *or there wouldn't be a second album… well, if there was and it was our choice of music, it wouldn't be getting their support. A joke, but we were pathetically accepting and the album got no support anyway.'*
> Simon Nelson

There's another point to be made here. Not least because you would expect to find a long list of demos like this at the back of this book.

Now, it's true that the Milltown Brothers and their associates may have started believing huge success was inevitable, that they were appalling at dealing with their record label, that they spent far too much time away from the UK than was healthy, and that they went on to make some appalling decisions – but they were always excellent songwriters, and it is to their eternal credit that they managed to demo well over 50 individual tracks before the end of 1992 in increasingly tough circumstances.

Half of the second album and several songs that are arguably superior to some tracks that appear on *Valve* – including 'Don't Breathe In', 'Rosemary Page', 'Drop Like A Stone' and 'Worldwide' – were demoed during 1991 and offered up for sacrifice. And the rest of the songs that appear on the album – bar the Dylan cover 'It's All Over Now, Baby Blue' – were around by August 1992, yet *Valve* still didn't appear for another year, well over two years after the release of *Slinky*.

Management

In the middle of this, the first of their four major music contracts came up for renewal. Their initial four-year management contract with Globeshine and Tim had come to a conclusion in autumn 1992. While the band were pretty vulnerable, they had several options open to them without having to cast the net further than existing relationships.

The most surprising – yet encouraging and exciting – was that A&M put forward John Reid to take over the management of the band. Described in *Music Week* in 2021 as *'brilliant'*, he was the manager of their label stablemates Del Amitri, and remained with them through thick and thin for 30 years until his retirement. At the very least, this demonstrated support from A&M and a belief that the Milltown Brothers retained potential. And that with a strong, experienced and trusted manager in place, they could sort it out.

Tim Paton also wanted to continue to manage the band. He felt he'd served his apprenticeship with Globeshine and the band for four years and knew they were plenty good enough. So much so, he wanted to end ties with Globeshine and start his own band management company with the Milltown Brothers as his standard bearer.

And there was a third option. Andy Proudfoot had been the band's tour manager for a year or so, since the first tour of America. He was a good tour manager, was popular with the band and eager to get into band management... but lacked any band management experience. He also had *'a few nice ideas about merchandising'*, details of which are long forgotten.

Nian is best placed to explain the difference between a tour and band manager, having gone on to do both quite a few years later. *'The two jobs couldn't be more different. A band manager manages all aspects of the band's career, liaising with the record company, publishing company and booking agent. They are the person in the middle, coordinating all the different areas of band activity, hopefully to an end goal based on a strategy that they have put together with the record company and band. The manager is the go-to for all the band...it literally involves looking after everything and anything. When things are going well, it's usually down to the band. When things are going badly, it's usually the fault of the manager! So a very tough job...a thankless task in many ways. They earn their 20 per cent. Whereas a tour manager is solely responsible for managing the logistics of a live tour/show. This mostly involves managing the budget, booking crew, booking travel and accommodation and then running the day-to-day business of the tour, very much operational; getting the band from A to B, taking them to radio/press promotional activity and finally getting them onstage and managing any* merchandise sales before and after the show. A tour manager plays no part in musical decisions etc., it's mostly just getting practical stuff done. Once a tour is finished, they aren't involved until the next one. They're paid a daily rate and have no percentage of band income.'

Given these three choices, what would you do? What would most people of sound mind do, given the band's past experiences and in a situation where they felt they'd not been able to communicate with their record company in the right way to create a balanced and even-handed relationship? Given too that there'd never been a plan put in place to make sure the right things happened at the right time and in the right places – so that less than a year after seemingly about to go huge, they had few apparent friends in A&M, were drifting out of the public eye, song after song after song was getting rejected and they'd not put out any new – or old – music in over a year and played only a handful of small headline gigs in the UK?

A&M surely wouldn't be suggesting a highly regarded manager of one of their major bands if they'd any doubts about either the quality of the person they were putting forward or the future of the Milltown Brothers. And if the band's manager was A&M's choice, you've got to believe everyone involved would be as one about getting the band centre stage and everything done to achieve that.

As regards Tim, little would be lost by him starting out on his own; the band had never seen much of Brian Hallin and he'd never struck them as particularly dynamic or charismatic. Starting on his own could be a strong motivation for him to work full-time, smarter and harder on behalf of the band and maybe get fresh management blood involved. He was significantly more experienced than he'd been four years earlier and he was a nice guy, one of the gang… but he wasn't a planner and maybe he'd reached the limits of his capabilities. Now that things had become tougher, he'd not been able to do much about it.

As for Andy, he was in more or less the same position Tim had been in when he first got involved with a much more

inexperienced Milltown Brothers in 1988, with very limited contacts in the music industry and certainly not at the level dealing
with A&M required.

None of this is easy, especially when you're young, full of
braggadocio, more or less on your own business-wise, you've had
your lives looked after up to this point, and the pressure is on.
But I have to report that the band in democratic fashion sensa-
tionally chose to make the future look decidedly worse than it
already was.

Nian voted for John Reid.
Matthew voted for Andy.
James voted for Andy.
Simon voted for John Reid.
And Barney voted for Andy.

Tim got no votes whatsoever, which was understandable and
reluctantly accepted by the band. He'd not been able to navigate
the difficulties of the last few months; there wasn't any clear strategy or plan and never had been.

Somehow Matthew, James and Barney ignored both the
wiser heads of Simon and Nian and the lessons of the past. Either
they were deeply seduced by Andy's merchandising ideas or they
had become sufficiently intimidated by the idea of being managed by someone A&M respected and had put forward that they
believed his first responsibility would be to A&M. A miserable
and dumb summation of how their relationship with them had
been allowed to develop, without any particularly wilful unpleas-
antness or disagreement on either side. They couldn't see beyond
a likely conflict of interest and didn't think band and label in
harmony was possible, never mind an ideal scenario.

And irrespective of how talented and capable Andy might
ever have been, he was completely out of his depth and on a
hiding to nothing. The damage may already have been done less
fortunately elsewhere, but to say the band were now pushing
their increasingly wretched luck in a manner that was completely

unnecessary is an understatement. Especially as they'd already been told in no uncertain terms by A&M that appointing Andy seemed like a very bad idea. Unsurprisingly, the decision amazed and infuriated A&M, who'd gone out on a limb to make things work for the band by getting John Reid involved and then had it thrown back in their faces.

Nian sums it up best: *'Even though I'm the least sentimental and most pragmatic in the band, I've subsequently been involved with precisely these tasks personally and I find it very difficult to think, never mind talk with anything approaching a level head about that decision. As I said at the time, it was like chopping your own leg off when you had the opportunity to not just keep it but let someone else do all the running for you and give you a helping hand if you needed it. We were struggling and a bit deranged is the best I can say about us. The reality is, appointing Andy was a double whammy, both a symptom and then a cause of our fall, just ridiculous... madness...'*

As for Tim, surely sticking with a friend who was indebted to them, was more experienced and at least known to A&M would have been a better second choice than giving the job to someone as raw as Andy? It remained an unfortunate and sad parting of the ways, although it was good for Tim. He emerged with his credibility intact, exonerated from any responsibility for the increasingly uncertain future for the band he had managed from nowhere to a debut album that entered the charts at 27 in three years, and a band that had toured America and Japan at a time when industry regard for it was high.

Romance

Wretchedly the band had yet another problem. They were spending less and less time together and hardly ever alone as a unit. Long term live-in girlfriends – and indeed wives – as part of the dynamic was a relatively new dimension in 1992, before which relationships had always been managed with the band as the absolute focus.

In and of itself, this wasn't divisive in terms of the people, their personalities or the relationships involved – everyone got on great when their partners turned up for demos, recordings and tours, unlike many more famous luminaries – but it did mean the bandmates spent much less time together and decisions were increasingly influenced by their relationships and personal circumstances, rather than what was in the best interests of the band.

The value of the gang, the utilitarian strength of the band's togetherness, was undermined, and there was still no plan or person in place against which to measure or judge the wisdom of any decisions. Ties among the band slackened. Their prime interest no longer rested with their bandmates, and they were living all over the place with their partners, putting more pressure on the music making, which became about organised sessions when the songs had to be forced and less about them organically emerging from loads of time being together as a way of life.

Simon, who had been in a relationship with Rachel since 1985, with only a brief break, got married in June 1992 in the village of Elton just outside Peterborough. The band all attended and played a handful of acoustic numbers.

Nian had been with his girlfriend, Suzanne, since school, but during the band's tour of Japan in February 1992 he met Joely, an American from Atlanta, Georgia. The relationship with Suzanne had been faltering for a while, and the arrival of Joely brought it to a close. Meeting her had been quite freakishly lucky – or unlucky – depending on your perspective. Dog-tired Nian had insisted he was going to bed despite the band having been invited to Lexington Queen to party with Bryan Adams et al. Barney dragged him out of bed. Joely was at the party, and the rest is history. She moved to the UK in September 1992, studied fashion at Central Saint Martins, moved into a small flat in Maida Vale with Nian, and they got married at Camden Registry office in October 1993 – just before Nian got his first paying job outside the band, while still being in the band – with Nobby and his partner Lee as witnesses.

James had met Gabriela, a Puerto Rican, in Boston at the Nirvana show in September 1991 and was besotted. He spent six months living in Bath with her and did the Charlatans' tour in April 1992, travelling by hired car with Gabriela rather than on the tour bus with the rest of the band. The two would eventually split up towards the end of 1993 after trying to maintain what had become a long-distance relationship – which was an emotional disaster for James.

Matthew had a girlfriend in America and wanted to spend time there when he could.

Barney was engaged to his longstanding English girlfriend from Burnley, Julie. But even this brought its stresses because he insisted on living up north while the rest of the band lived, more or less, in various parts of London.

'It wasn't in any way difficult or awkward,' explains Nian, *'everyone got on, but it just wasn't the same… that tight-knit group of lads just doing our thing, the music and stuff. 1992 was jaded, a more distant version of that thing. We never fell out, but we were much less in a groove, together. Before, we didn't have to work at that, it's just what we wanted to do, then… relationships… distractions embraced with open arms… we inevitably started to want different things and hardly ever spent any time alone unless we planned it and it felt forced and formal and demanded outputs. We were almost friendly strangers at times with our heads always turned slightly away.'*

One of James' few regrets about the Milltown Brothers experience is that they never used any of their income to buy their own recording equipment and studio space. Apart from his personal interest, it would have given them a much better chance to continue to spend time in a studio together, make music organically. It might even have carried them through this period and the increasingly mind-numbing times that followed when they were less and less in demand. Certainly, it would have put them in a much better position to make and release music cost effectively when things hit rock bottom.

More Off Than On

The band were never really anything but just about on the road again. They found it difficult to adjust to playing smaller shows with scantier, less fervent followers. The ten gigs supporting the Charlatans in bigger venues in April was a brief highlight, but the festival bits and pieces and half-dozen smaller headline shows in August and September 1992, notably supported by Cast at the Muni, Colne, were a step down and followed a disastrous headline spot at a free festival stacked with local bands in Oak Hill Park in Accrington, close to Burnley.

Anne-Marie Smith in the band's UK fanzine, *Coming From The Mill*, tells the story. *'The day gets off to a bad start when technical problems delay proceedings by well over an hour and with a feeble and very dodgy P.A. the only good thing is that it wasn't raining.*

'After six bands have taken the tiny stage and some folks have packed up and gone home, the Milltowns came on to perform a very dismal 20 minutes that mixed new stuff with old favourites in-between at which point Matt throws down his microphone in frustration leaving Simon to fill in lead vocals on songs such as 'Here I Stand' and 'Sleepwalking'. Each time they busk their way out of trouble to produce neat little endings that no one seemed bothered about anyway, I think this was half the problem.

'No one stood up apart from the guy shouting out obscenities and no one screamed their approval apart from one girl yelling in my left ear. You get the feeling the band just aren't used to being ignored anymore, leaving all that behind them now and not before time. They've got a succession of beautifully crafted songs at their fingertips and a sussed stage presence – when they're in the mood.

'As for today's efforts, Matt sings way out of tune and drones "This one's called 'Apple Green'" as if he couldn't give a toss. Six songs later he's had enough and walks off stage, leaving the others to mop up and follow him. A warmup for Reading? Things didn't even get tepid.'

Reading 1992 in front of 20,000 on the main stage followed. Nirvana were now headlining and closing the festival on Sunday while the Milltown Brothers were way down the bill on Friday, much more last year's thing than the band who'd *'cracked it'* in 1991 just eight months earlier.

The two-sentence *NME* review of 5 September 1992, edited by Steve Lamacq – but dismissively and inaccurately written by Gina Morris – said it all. *'The Milltown Brothers, however, have simply forgotten to bring their bow and arrows and even if they had they wouldn't have been able to hit a dead pigeon with today's insipid performance. I don't like one sentence dismissals but if 39,999 people can choose to ignore them so can I.'*

With such a resounding endorsement communicated to the music world, the band managed a handful more small gigs before – finally – 'Turn Off' was released in May 1993, the follow-up to 'Apple Green'… just the small matter of 22 months later.

'Turn Off'

'Turn Off' had originally been demoed, then produced by Gil Norton in October 1992 and really was the only song approved by A&M during the whole of that year. Gil had worked with Echo & the Bunnymen, Martin Stephenson, the Pixies, Del Amitri and on 'Sit Down' with James. The band loved his approach and were keen to work with him on the second album, but having produced 'Turn Off' he couldn't or wouldn't commit to do the album, which was disappointing. Whatever his reasons, it felt like further evidence of the decline of the band's fortunes.

The 7" vinyl was backed with 'Worldwide', the 12" vinyl and CD 1 in addition had 'Got This Feeling', while CD2 had three completely different tracks: 'Caroline', 'Rosemary Page' and 'Alice'. None of these tracks would end up on *Valve*.

As for the artwork, the best way to sum it up is as an idea that was pretty random, unoriginal and open for unhelpful interpretations a hammer in the act of striking a nail.

'Turn Off'

Here's a line why don't you start it,
How's it feel now you've crossed it,
Starve a cold to feed a habit,
Don't tell me that's part of growing up.

There it goes again, messing up my friend.

Better turn off, don't do that again,
Turn off, don't do that again,
Turn off, don't do that again,
Turn off, don't do that again.

Hard to stop what's been started,
Headlines say you've been discarded,
There's no colour in your lover,
Lies disguise another cover up.

There it goes again, messing up my friend.

Better turn off, don't do that again,
Turn off, don't do that again,
Turn off, don't do that again,
Turn off, don't do that again.

The time you waste will bring you down,
And you can't slow down,
The way it brings you down,
And I don't know why, you don't know why.

There's a line why don't you stop it,
Maybe even try to get off it,
Even now I know you want it,
All I wish, I wish you'd shut up.

There it goes again, messing up my friend.

Better turn off, don't do that again,
Turn off, don't do that again,
Turn off, don't do that again,
Turn off, don't do that again.

Turn off, don't do that again,
Turn off, don't do that again,
Turn off, don't do that again,
Turn off, don't do that again.

There was a little Radio 1 daytime airplay, but the single was largely ignored by the music media – one review in *Time Out* and a Radio 5 session with Mark Radcliffe on *Hit The North,* when 'Killing All The Good Men, Jimmy', 'Turn Off', 'Sleepwalking' and 'Turn Me Over' were the highlights.

It did manage to limp into the charts at 55. Indulging in a spot of wishful thinking, Simon likes to think if it had been called 'Turn On' it might have done much better.

Significantly the most noteworthy press came in a brief column in the *Daily Star*'s entertainment gossip column, regarding the band's refusal – notwithstanding Nian's occasionally bare upper torso – to strip off for the mildly salacious video produced in support of the single.

The band present themselves with a dark, prescient boy band saturnine glossiness and a moody almost lounge lizard demeanour, complete with slick haircuts, primped and sharply styled black leather – but this was interspersed not with the band doing other stuff but with scantily clad models pouring various viscous liquids over themselves and revelling in the pleasure.

The models were much more comfortable in significantly less clothes than the band, but it was all rather tired – misogynistic, cliched and stereotypical to the point of arguably being a remake of Robert Palmer's 'Addicted to Love', a bizarre video that was immensely effective at the time (1985). That said, the models featured in the band's video at least appear to be more adept at pouring viscous liquid over themselves than those in 'Addicted to Love' were at playing their instruments.

The band embarked on a disjointed 15-date tour of the UK to promote 'Turn Off', opening at Loughborough University on 29 April and culminating in a sold-out gig at Burnley Mechanics in June 1993.

'It's All Over Now, Baby Blue'

Suddenly things were happening too quickly. In July, and against the wishes of the band, who wanted 'Falling Straight Down' to be the next single, A&M released the Dylan cover they'd been forced to record, courtesy of Harold Berman. Matthew dislikes singing other people's songs and is no fan of covers, even when the song is Bob's.

It was backed with 'Sweet Nothing' on the 7" single – their reworking of the Spire's 'Salford Lady' from 1986. The 10" vinyl and two CDs were issued with alternative B-sides: CD1 had three (more or less) pre-A&M singles, 'Roses', 'Which Way Should I Jump?' and 'Seems To Me', while CD2 and the 10" vinyl featured three different supporting tracks – all Dylan covers ('Hurricane', 'Positively 4th Street' and 'I Shall Be Released'), recorded in May 1993 at Out of The Blue, Ancoats, Manchester. Other than the somewhat dull 'I Shall Be Released', the covers are plenty good enough, if somewhat poignant in a couple of their titles.

You might even think it was some sort of closing down sale.

'...obscurity beckons' – the surprising yet brief *Independent* review finished thus. But it's a great Milltown Brothers song. They don't like it because of how it came about, what it came to represent, the unfortunate title and the decline it marked in their fortunes... and it's a cover. But it did better than 'Turn Off', making 48 in the charts, and the official video is perhaps the best the band made.

It's a 'pop art' performance returning the band to a more

innocent, joyous, open-hearted and less cynical time, with the knowing boyish charms of the band circa 1989/1990. It's colourful, bright and almost carefree alongside a subtle undercurrent of pathos, as the band weave a little magic in and among representations of various pop art icons, including Andy Warhol, Divine and Lichtenstein, with Matthew briefly morphing into a couple of pop artworks, emulating Elvis and your choice of Warhol celebrity – let's go with Marilyn Monroe – along the way. It also gave fans a unique opportunity to see Barney strumming an acoustic guitar.

Valve

With now reckless haste and abandon, the Milltown Brother's second album was finally released in early August 1993. It was for Simon *'the offspring of a long, drawn-out and deeply unpleasant process which essentially traced our journey from within touching distance of the top to scratching around on the bottom… who'd have thought that's how I'd describe putting together our second album five years ago when simply making an album was our idea of incredible success?'*

For Matthew: *'Just a procession of instruments not a band.'*

And for Nian: *'An absolute mishmash riddled with a relentless snare reverb.'*

Along with the struggles to satisfy A&M, the band had never found a producer they were happy with. By now, they had worked their way through Mick Glossop (who'd given Simon a hard time), Dave Meegan, Gil Norton (to their disappointment), and Ian Brodie of the Lightning Seeds (who simply turned the offer to produce their album down), so A&M gave them Chris Sheldon, originally one of Gil Norton's engineers, and insisted they get the album done. They had an album to record, and they'd be doing it in Livingston Studios in Wood Green, North London, within just a few dark, wet and cold weeks in January and February 1993.

Chris would go on to have a hugely successful career with the likes of Therapy?, Shed Seven and Biffy Clyro – and also mixed and engineered The Pixies single 'Dig for Fire' in 1990, which will forever hold a place in my heart. He doesn't mention *Valve* in his long and detailed list of credits on Wikipedia, but he did a remarkable job to cobble it together from a number of sources and recordings. Obviously he was given a brief to get the band in and out of the studio as quickly as possible, with minimal support and cost… and if the result happened to do okay, A&M would take it from there; or if, as expected, it bombed, A&M could simply write off the whole thing and the band as a tax loss and move on. The production information on the album demonstrates what this amounted to:

'1 when it comes 2 turn off 3 killing all the good men, jimmy 4 pictures (round my room) 5 turn me over 6 trees 7 sleepwalking 8 falling straight down 9 crawl with me 10 someday 11 it's all over now baby blue 12 cool breeze. TRACK 1, 3, 5, 10, 11, 12 PRODUCED BY CHRIS SHELDON. TRACK 2 PRODUCED BY GIL NORTON, ENGINEERED BY PETE WOODRUFFE. TRACKS 4, 7, 9 PRODUCED BY DAVE MEEGAN. TRACKS 6 & 8 PRODUCED BY MICK GLOSSOP. TRACK 2, 4, 6, 7, 9 MIXED BY CHRIS SHELDON. TRACK 8 ADDITIONAL PRODUCTION AND MIX BY CHRIS SHELDON'

The album was dedicated to the memory of Spike and there were a couple of surprising inclusions in the sleeve notes: a long dedication to Amnesty International on the basis of the inclusion of 'Killing All The Good Men, Jimmy' and a handwritten disjointed ramble by Matthew having a go at various band demons without pointing the finger directly at anyone.

As to the title of the album, it's certainly an improvement on *Slinky*, and quietly something of a cry for help and yelp of relief. The band tell me it's the dual idea of a life-giving heart with its valves and chambers, and the release of pressure a valve delivers when opened.

The cover art is terrible. It has little to do with the album title or content, other than having a T-shirt and badge with a V on it. It's extremely hard to find any irony in it either, and it

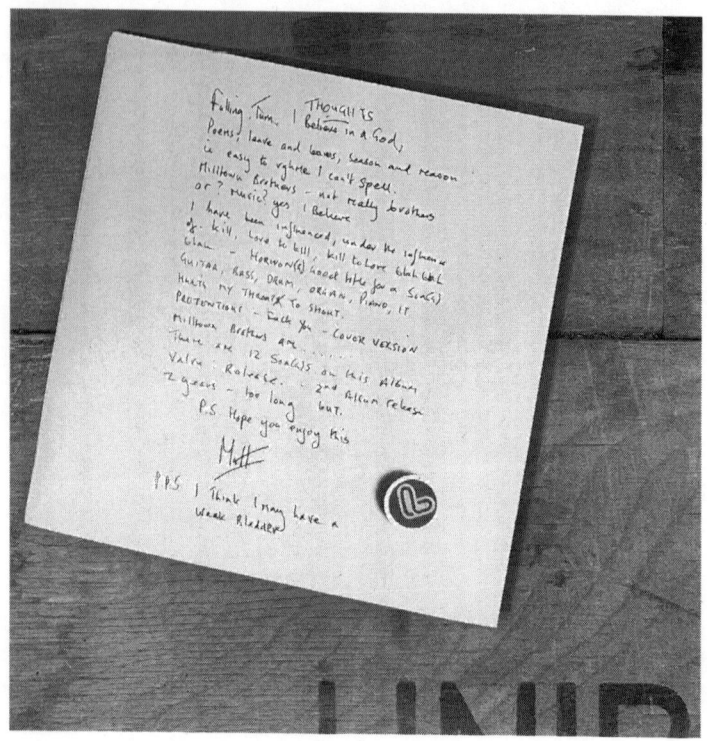

Matthew rambling on *Valve*

is only superficially worked through the rest of the artwork via a handful of black and white music pin badges. It features the mid torso – neck to crotch – of a young guy dressed in double denim fresh out of the packet, and bears no relation whatsoever to the moody monotone shots within of band members clad in leather and black. The denim jacket is festooned with a jumbled array of colourful and iconic pin badges, mostly relating to pop and rock music but rather tacky, although they do include the Milltown Brothers' Stanley figure, a Blue Peter badge, the Amnesty International logo and some political sloganeering, alongside the T-shirt and badge with V for Valve and – James suggests somewhat oddly – Vagina.

It desperately seems to be trying to associate the band with – very loosely – pop art and, more directly, a vintage rock 'n' roll lineage, a juvenile catch-all idea, badly and embarrassingly executed, such that it looks like someone painfully trying to be trendy and cool when they self-evidently aren't. The band assure me the artwork had little to do with them.

What about the music? Well, despite the frustrations and band's unhappiness with the album, there are some wonderful songs on *Valve*, even if they're not always ideally represented by the version that appears on it. There are a couple of fillers – 'Crawl With Me' and 'Someday' – but songs like 'When It Comes', 'Killing All The Good Men, Jimmy', 'Pictures (Round My Room)', 'Falling Straight Down' and 'Cool Breeze' (which the band had to fight hard to get on the album in the first place) all have the potential to be great singles, in addition to the three tracks that were quickly released as singles – and they have stood the test of time.

Valve was woefully unsupported by A&M and ignored by the music press. Reviews were for the most part negative and probably written to a prescribed brief, or without listening to the album much, if at all. A few – *Record Mirror* ('But for once they transcend the tricky second album syndrome with a record which swaggers with power, verve and confidence') and some of the more mainstream press – provided more balanced perspectives. But the band were just not flavour of any month.

Yet having got the album out, they still hoped it could surprise them, Lazarus-like. They bigged it up in the press on the rare occasion they got the chance, then waited.

They were playing the legendary – if small – Duchess of York in Leeds on 5 August 1993, when they received the news *Valve* had debuted in the charts at 103. Dead in the water. And they still had a ragged 20-date tour to endure in support of it, playing venues similar to those they'd been playing in 1988 and 1989.

This included a gig at Manchester Hop & Grape, the smallest venue in Manchester University. Originally scheduled for 1 October 1993, it took place on the 14th. They were supported by the Real People – who didn't make the gig – and another band that had been formed only two years earlier by the Gallagher brothers from Manchester, had just signed to Alan McGee's Creation Records and were now starting to put together their first album. *Definitely Maybe*, the first album by Oasis would be released less than a year later, go on to top the UK album charts for weeks, be certified a nine times platinum seller in the UK and sell over 15 million copies worldwide.

'Sleepwalking'

Meanwhile, on 6 September and unbeknown to the band, the Milltown Brothers had released their third single of 1993. It's far from being the most obvious choice on the album for a single, but no one seemed to care, although the lyrics were prescient. Was someone at A&M having the last laugh?

'Sleepwalking'

And I'd like to sleepwalk through your life
And spend my time just watching
I'd like to stare at people rushing by
As they pass, they seem to wonder why
This could be the end
This could be the end

This could be the end of what we started
Now we're trying to forget
And all the reasons why we started
We're beginning to regret

Funny how my words just don't apply
When I talk to you and you talk to me
As if this was the end
This could be the end

This could be the end of what we started
Now we're trying to forget
And all the reasons why we started
We're beginning to regret

Never really want to be there
Never really want to be there

Would you like to sleepwalk through my life
Who's that talking in my mind
Words like whirlpools lost in time
I'm spinning, I'm falling, I'm drowning, I'm learning
This could be the end
This could be the end

It got no support, no video, received no airplay and no reviews, the pop equivalent of a gold rush town after the gold has gone. This was the first Milltown Brothers single not to chart since the independent release of 'Which Way Should I Jump?' over four years earlier in 1989. It was issued as a 7" vinyl – backed by 'Fee Fie Foe Fum', a much better song than its title suggests – and a couple of CD singles, one with 'Fee Fie Foe Fum', 'You Don't Know Me No More' and 'Long Time' in support, the other with 'Everybody Knows', 'Can't Find the Time' and 'Freedom Song'.

Dropped

On the day 'Sleepwalking' was released, the Milltown Brothers still had a publishing company, a booking agent, a manager and a record label.

EMI had done pretty well from their publishing deal with the band, not just with the radio airplay and TV appearances. Their songs continued to appear regularly on several prime-time programmes, including *London's Burning*, *Coronation Street* and *EastEnders* – 'Which Way Should I Jump?' being a particular favourite in the Bridge Street Café, while 'Apple Green' was deemed more appropriate to the Queen Vic jukebox – and a variety of sports programmes and highlight reels. They decided not to take up the option of extending the deal after the first album, but in July 1993, around the time of the release of 'It's All Over Now, Baby Blue', Rondor, sister company of A&M, surprisingly took up the publishing contract and paid the band a not inconsiderable advance of £70,000.

As for the band's booking agent, it was still Primary, who had supplanted Concorde when the band were on the up. Their contact, Nigel Hassler believed in the Milltown Brothers and was still getting them gigs and promising to continue to do so. Which is where the good news ends.

'Your carriage clock's in the post.'

That's how Andy Proudfoot jauntily announced the loss of their most important asset. In what was perhaps the defining moment of his handling of the band, he rang them in turn to explain they no longer had a record company, having been dropped by A&M on 13 September 1993, the moment 'Sleepwalking' failed to chart. At which point the band still had the larger part of the ragged album tour in front of them, including the Oasis gig.

This was a cause for an outbreak of glee and hilarity at *NME*. In their next issue they ran a photograph of a joyous office party described as the A & R department at A&M celebrating the dropping of the Milltown Brothers.

Planned and premeditated as it was, A&M's decision was short-sighted in the light of what then happened: a reaction to grunge, which prompted the renaissance of guitar bands in the UK. Britpop, spearheaded by the rivalry between Blur and Oasis, meant bands such as Suede, Pulp, Shed Seven, Cast, Elastica and Ocean Colour Scene, all with relatively meaningless names, had their day in the sun – and, in a few cases, a whole lot more – but A&M didn't see this coming and neither did the band.

Simon says now: *'If we'd just stuck it out as the Milltown Brothers for another year or two, looked around a bit, stopped feeling sorry for ourselves, stopped being screwed up by perceived injustices and our luck collapsing and got back to grafting on the road and making less expensive music, which we could easily have done – it's what we loved doing underneath it all – we might have got back involved when Blur and Oasis crossed swords. We had the songs, we just needed to suffer, but we couldn't see that coming and the truth is we all eventually thought life was passing us by and gave in. A&M was dead, they were probably over a million pounds down and another album made no sense to them, but the alternative of going back to square one with maybe an indie label was there. The problem was if that failed, the idea of ending up in our 30s with absolutely nothing to show for it and having to start again is what really finished us off… Barney wanting out wasn't good for us, but we could have toughed it out… we didn't and our bruised heads still had a part to play.'*

Last In, First Out

The band laid down their first demos for Rondor at their studio in London – 'Career', 'Us' (originally from the Mick Glossop session in 1992), 'Water in Our Lungs', 'Freeze Frame' and 'Anything' – and ploughed on with the *Valve* tour while Andy unsuccessfully did what he could to find them a new record company.

A letter appeared in the *NME* bemoaning the '*much ignored demise*' of the Milltown Brothers.

With the band meandering grimly along as the tour tamely drew towards its conclusion in October 1993, Barney was the first to decide to do something else. After all, when he had first bumped into Matthew in their shared bathroom, he was about to study Business because he hadn't the qualifications, expertise or experience for what he really wanted to do: music. He was now in a much better position to go back to Plan A, and hoped that what he'd been doing might mean the qualifications weren't required. It was still a shock when he announced he was leaving a fortnight after they'd been supported by Oasis, on the penultimate night of the tour at Derby University on 29 October 1993. With a certain serendipity, ergo luck, Leeds College of Music had just launched a degree course in Jazz that autumn, and Barney fully intended being part of the second intake the next year.

Nian was next to do something else without leaving the band. During much of 1992, he'd been socialising with Simon's friends who were six or seven years out of university and earning spectacular salaries, while the band were still drawing their £400 monthly from all but depleted advances. The deal with Rondor made a big difference in the short term, but they were frittering it away and paying off some accumulated debts, and without a recording contract the band was likely to be history. As the one most likely to need money first, given that his parents had none to speak of and he was in London and freshly married to Joely, who was studying fashion and would be for a while, he wasn't keen on hanging around in the hope something would fall their way, but he didn't want to leave the band eithers. He thought at the level they were now operating he could combine drumming with this thing called a day job. *'It was no longer a case of the band being a career choice, that had long gone, I came to realise I couldn't be messing about with a band forever...'*

In 18 months the band had fallen from the brink to less than it had been in 1987 – *'messing about with a band'* – and Nian applied for a job in the *Evening Standard* as a flat letting agent with a company called Black Katz based in Camden – the band's old stomping ground. To his surprise, he got it. More surprising still, he loved the nine-to-five from day one – he'd got lucky again. As the name suggests, Black Katz was not a typical letting agency, more a modern, chilled one where you wore a T-shirt and jeans and gave off a certain youthful, cool and vibrant air. It was a match made in heaven, and Nian couldn't have been better qualified. Not only did he get the job, he was good at it. The owners, a handful of years older than him, shared his outlook and were friends with the people who launched Heavenly Records in 1990. In other words, Nian landed on his feet and loved waking up with a purpose rather than the *'waiting for the next thing to happen'* associated with being in a band. He was given a car, and every time he let a property, he earned £400, matching his monthly band salary.

Simon, Matthew and James were more reluctant to give up on the dream. They ploughed on in relative austerity with Nian still along for the ride, but the dole was increasingly their sole source of income. In and among growing periods of boredom, irritation, inactivity, introspection, heavy drinking and tears, they spasmodically tried to get something going – a day at Rondor Studios producing 'Breathe Easy', 'God Is A Girl', 'Oxygen' and 'Something For Nothing'.

They were wrestling with this tarnished broken thing called the Milltown Brothers, balancing the residual value of being known against making a fresh start. They were, after all, no longer quite the same band and were writing darker songs, which could expose them again to accusations of 'Seems To Me'-style shapeshifting to find fans. James was playing lead guitar with Simon on bass. Doubts about the name had never quite been put to bed and were now front of mind, amplified by the punchbag they'd become for the press when it had nothing else to write about. It wasn't just the likes of *NME* who were having a go; even the north-west journalists who'd always gloried in the exploits of their bunch of local lads done well, saw them as fair game. A now unknown regional reporter was more than happy to raise a spiky old issue or two during a telephone interview with the band. *'Don't you think the Mill Owners would have been a more appropriate name than the Milltown Brothers?'* But they still had Rondor, they still had Primary, and they still had Andy.

Andy discussed the idea of the band changing their name with Primary, but Nigel Hassler was insistent they stick to their guns and hang in there: their time could come again, he saw the signs, they were the Milltown Brothers, a name change could only deliver obscurity.

At the same time another fragile, watery shard of light bore fruit when, as previously explained, 'Here I Stand' was chosen as the theme music for *All Quiet on the Preston Front*, the BBC comedy drama. This was surely their moment. But they managed to screw that up too. Not only did they miss out commercially by short-sightedly accepting a one-off payment for licensing 'Here I Stand' for use throughout the lifespan of the programme, they couldn't see the positives or the potential of the exposure and had neither the confidence, balls nor manager to approach A&M and discuss rereleasing 'Here I Stand'. Since the series developed a big following and received widespread acclaim, that wasn't... clever.

And even when they were handed a gilt-edged opportunity to remind a nationwide audience how good they were – an invitation on the daytime BBC programme *Pebble Mill*, hosted by a relatively youthful Alan Titchmarsh and Judi Spiers – they either couldn't be bothered or were trying something new. They're not sure themselves what they were doing.

Either way, the band including Barney turned up and managed to play 'Here I Stand'. But it was almost a dirge. They appeared physically and psychologically disengaged and numb, as if they couldn't care less. No one in the band smiles, moves or catches one another's gaze. Barney uncharacteristically skulks in the background. Matthew is pale, unshaven and lank haired, looking as scrawny as he's ever done under a baker boy cap, and buried by a long, button-up, black leather jacket. Staring dolefully down the camera lens and punctuating his gaze by occasionally opening his eyes wide – the most demonstrative movement of the band's performance – he sings in a deep, querulous, half-shout monotone, frequently off when pitching for the higher notes, his arms wrapped protectively around himself. At the end there is a hint of a wry smile as he turns away from the 'applause'. It conjures up comparisons with the dramatic transformation in Depeche Mode from a synth teeny bopper band to a thing of grimmer, heavier hue around the same time. Judi Spiers tries to lighten the tone by making a self-effacing joke, referring to Matthew as the lead singer rather than his name, which she appears to have forgotten. '*I got all excited you know when the lead singer asked me for my signed autograph and I thought, You've still got it, Spiers... and then he said, No, it's for my father...*'

A short tour of the Netherlands followed at the end of January 1994: four gigs and a radio session. Proof that Nigel Hassler at Primary was still able to deliver. They played Amsterdam, the Hague, Leiden and Uden and revisited Hilversum, where they'd played a storming two-song session in 1990 – 'Here I Stand' and 'Apple Green'. This time it was 'Dirty Girl', 'Silly Thing', 'Cinderella Jones' and the final song from *Slinky*, 'Cool Breeze'. Peter Perrett and the Only Ones were on the session too, and to Simon's delight played the new wave classic 'Another Girl, Another Planet'.

The band's only booked gigs in the next couple of months were at the Carlton Inn in Morecambe and Rock Garden in Covent Garden. The Milltown Brothers featuring all original five members – Simon, Matthew, James, Barney and Nian – played the Carlton Inn in Morecambe on 17 May. It was a mix of songs, old and new, but mainly old, with Simon and James switching between playing lead guitar and bass throughout, a relatively happy upbeat night that went down well with a decent enough local crowd, despite it being a Tuesday in a tired seaside town.

The same five young men then did two demo sessions at Rondor Studios. At this point they had decided to call themselves Another Crush, and they demoed four songs: 'Silly Thing', 'Little Brown Drug', 'Domestic War' and 'Cinderella Jones'. The second session was by a band now calling itself Kingsize Screamer, which demoed 'A Lot Like Love', 'Outskirts of Newmarket' and '*a desperately dour nervous breakdown of a song*', 'Kingsize Screamer'. A day before the Rock Garden show, the band called Rondor to book another day to work on more new songs. The secretary, who knew them well, explained they couldn't because they no longer had a deal with Rondor. Their contract had been terminated and they weren't told.

It was Kingsize Screamer who played the last booked gig at Rock Garden on 2 June 1994. It was a mix of songs old and new, but mainly new, with James and Simon switching between lead guitar and bass throughout. It was a dark, desperate, miserable night for the band and a scanty crowd, despite it being a lovely sunny evening outside. Barney was mortified but he, at least, was in a fortunate position. When Nigel Hassler from Primary discovered the name change was permanent, he dropped them instantly and they never heard from him again.

As Andy Proudfoot had quietly disappeared to earn some money after the Netherlands tour, there was now nothing bar three blokes in a completely unknown band with a part-time drummer and not much money, nowhere to play, no one to help them and nothing to do.

It was just over six years since Steve Lamacq had bumped into the bright and refreshing pop with bollocks of the Milltown Brothers across the capital at the Bull & Gate in Kentish Town.

INTERLUDE — FANZINES

Predigital fanzines are things of painstaking, persistent wonder. Gloriously basic, crudely printed magazines, produced by fans for fans. A means of contacting and sharing. The further you go back, the more rudimentary the means of production and distribution. The more pressing the need, the more wonderful the fanzine. Pop and rock music fanzines appeared in the 1960s, then the format exploded with the DIY culture of Punk in the late '70s. *Sniffin' Glue* and *Ripped & Torn* were just two among thousands.

By the time Kerry Wadsworth and Debbie Murrell produced the first issue of the Milltown Brothers fanzine *Coming From The Mill* – with an old typewriter and photocopier – in April 1991, technology had moved on significantly. But it wasn't until issue No.4 that Debbie announced she'd managed to buy a word processor with the proceeds of the first three issues and help of '*a much appreciated contribution*'. Which was both nice and smart. If only the band could have been similarly smart elsewhere. The word processor didn't appear to have any impact on the appearance or quality of the fanzine, but it did get bigger. Issue No.1 had 20 pages, while No.9 had 56.

The inherent reality of fanzines is they're invariably just behind and outside of what's going on. They have to speculate on the thinnest of information, even when the object of their existence gets involved. The Milltown Brothers contributed from issue No.4, but for all manner of reasons – including the band often not having a clue either – information of any significance, beyond each of the band members' favourite songs, food and colour, was limited.

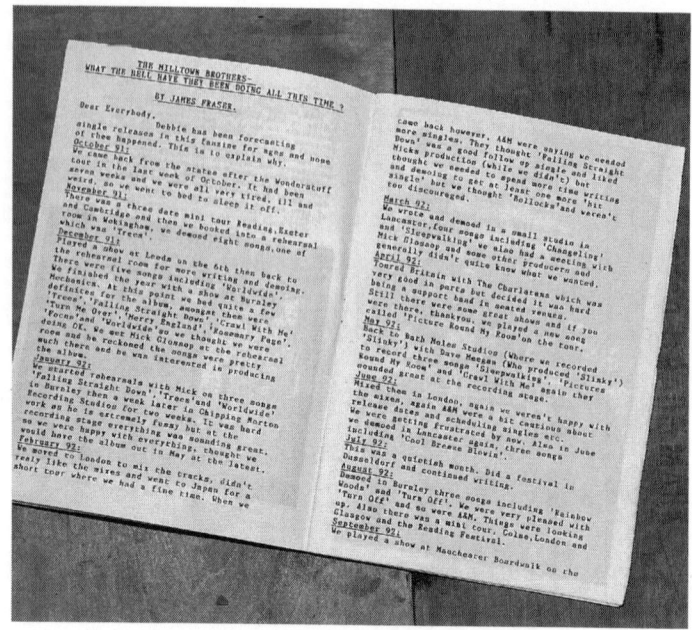

James' litany of excuses for no new tunes

An example. The date of the next Milltown Brothers single after the rereleased 'Apple Green' in July 1991 was wrongly predicted in issue No.3 – January 1992; issue No.5 – Summer 1992; and No.6 – January 1993, such that in No.7 James wrote a three-page article explaining why. Even then he said 'Turn Off' would be the next single in March. It was released in May.

All of this demands I slipped fanzines between Parts 4 and 5 of this book. Which neatly describes their life cycle too. Because they usually disappear with the dream, having not got started until the dream is well on the way.

The prerequisites for a fanzine?

Fans so into you they want to do it and so bloody-minded they see it through – with some history to rake through, future events to ponder, limited resources and a few points of view. And enough other fans to buy it.

No.1 April 1991

Kerry Wadsworth (editor) *'Being the first issue you may find it a bit thin on the ground...'*

No.2 July 1991

No.3 October 1991

Debbie Murrell takes over as editor from Kerry as she has *'decided to call it a day.'*

No.4 January 1992

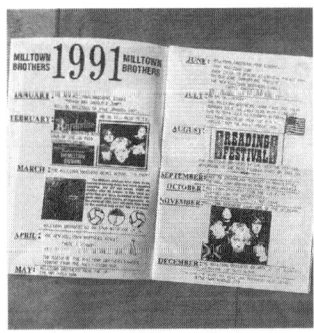

Barney on Matthew: *'slightly dozy sometimes but good at what he does.'*

Debbie intriguingly to Kerry. *'I don't really know what to say cos for one I couldn't fit it all in and two we both think we are right but sorry seems as good a start as any.'*

Nigel Wood

No.5 June 1992

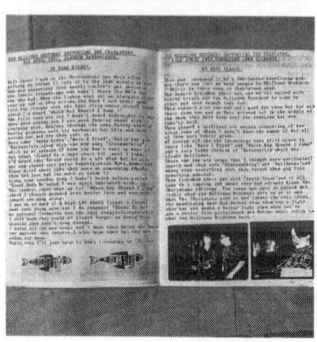

No.6 September 1992
'Nothing worth reproducing, a vacuous, long-winded issue with the most insipid cover.' Nigel Wood

No.7 January 1993

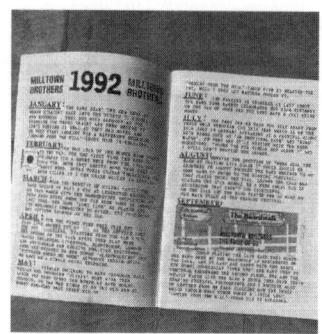

No.8 May 1993
Debbie: *'The Milky Bars are on me!!! Our cause for celebration being the brand new Milltown Brothers single as advertised opposite, the second album just around the corner and a UK tour happening as we speak. Not to mention the great new cover for 'Coming From The Mill' which was long overdue...'*

No.9 September 1993

> *'If we don't have a hit by May next year I'll eat all 9 copies of 'CFTM' for breakfast.'* Andy Proudfoot, *Coming From The Mill*, September 1993.

Debbie. *'Issue 10 will be available for £1.20 from erm, well erm, as soon as it's finished...'*

It was never finished. But let's not close on a sad note. Of all the questions answered by the band during the life of the fanzine, the most surprising answer was the following in No.8:

> *Debbie. 'Which band would you like to have as your tour support for the next tour?'* Barney. *'Iron Butterfly.'*

Most of you will ask who? Iron Butterfly were a psychedelic organ-driven American rock band from the 1960s, which I thought most people – and certainly anyone younger than me, like Barney – would never have heard of. On further investigation Barney's dad had the album *In-A-Gadda-Da-Vida* and he was deadly serious about wanting them to tour with the Milltown Brothers. They did reform in 1987, so this was not as unrealistic as it might appear.

There were two other fanzines, both from Japan. *Mill board* and *Never Come Down Again*. They lasted one and three issues respectively.

Mill-board remarkably appeared only four months after the first issue of *Coming From The Mill*. The band had not yet played in Japan. It's 12 pages mostly in Japanese with a page in English with 'key facts' about the boys. Matthew's favourite food is pies and he wants to make the band last forever. Nian wants to keep drifting like Bob Dylan. It was produced by Tomoko and Tokiko, who were among several Japanese fans who wrote richly ornate and visually beautiful letters to the band.

Never Come Down Again appeared in 1993 and ran for three issues, subtitled *'milltown brothers info. service in Japan'*. The

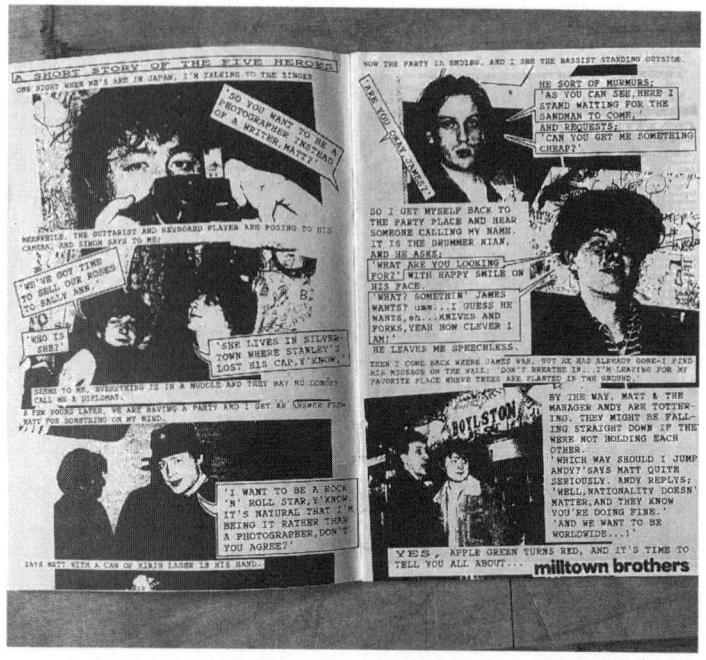

That picture story

creator, Ryoko Kawaoka, had followed the band around the UK for a year during 1990. The first issue is remarkably informative and well informed, including early music press clippings, a discography, brief history of the band, a diary of the 1992 Japanese tour and a Q&A. But it starts with an excruciating picture story about the band with as many Milltown Brothers song titles as possible in the dialogue. I can only speculate this catered to Japanese tastes.

The third issue closed with a poignant message to the band from Ryoko:

'One of my resolutions for '94 is to make another three Never Come Down Again's *by the end of the year and hopefully one of them will feature your 2nd Japan Tour. You've been waiting too long and so have I. 'All things come to him who wait'? Let's hope for a bright future!!'*

Part 5
LIGHT (1994–2025)

Matthew paused for a few seconds, labouring with the boot.
'Me in the Milltown Brothers?' He looked up.
'I think I still am.'

27

A pale, slightly out of shape, fair-haired bloke dressed in Next's interpretation of slim fit black jeans, plain white T and dark blue jacket is on his way to his first day in a new job: the footwear department at Next on Oxford Street, the busiest shopping street in Europe. The clothes are not quite with him; he looks like he's walking despite them, rather than with them.

He's 28 and it's 1996.

He feels terrible. Head bowed in misery, with a good dusting of shame. He's frightened of what lies ahead. Can't quite believe it's come to this, being really nice and even subservient to people and selling shoes. Exchanging pleasantries. It's not something he'd remotely considered he might ever have to do. He'd never even considered how to go about earning a living until recently.

He should be thankful he's got past that age, 27. Even though it had been a terrible year for him, he's been lucky. Much luckier than Kurt Cobain, for example. But he's not thinking that right now.

Right now, he's penniless and a new student, at 28. A kept man needing to make a contribution. And being ridiculously polite is a strange place for him, despite his nature and upbringing. He is little short of panic-stricken in a long, drawn-out yawning type of way. If the ground isn't willing to open and swallow him up before he arrives at the shop, all he really wants to do is skulk in the stockroom for 10 hours. But that isn't something Next want him to do; they think he could be a star when it comes to selling shoes and are happy to pay him to find out.

Going to work at Next straight from school is one thing. Coming from a very different place over 10 years later, as a student, quite another.

He'd been on the shop floor for almost two hours, studiously looking into the middle distance and finding things to do that enabled him to deal with only those people whose appearance suggested they wouldn't have come across him before – however likely or unlikely the possibility in a busy Oxford Street sense. But the shop was getting crowded and despite its dimensions hiding places were increasingly scarce.

A girl in her mid-20s was holding a leather boot up limply between the thumb and index finger of her right hand, looking around for someone like him, with a glum but open look on her face. Unable to find anyone else remotely like him who was obviously available, she decided he would have to do and gestured to him.

As he approached the girl, he tried to keep eye contact to a minimum, looking at the boot while having this sapping feeling she was spending an inordinate amount of time studying him, for someone who simply wished to try on – as it turned out – a pair of size 6s. But he would think that, wouldn't he?

'Hello, how are you doing, can I help with those?'

'Oh, yes… good thanks… thank you, er… could I try these on in a 6 please?'

'Of course, I'll just go and check… they've been very popular, be with you shortly, please grab a seat.'

'They've been very popular' was a wretched twisted struggle, it forced its way out. He wandered off but was back all too shortly, easing the right boot out of the box as he noticed her shoeless right foot. Kneeling in front of her with his head bowed, grateful the boots didn't have laces to deal with, he glanced up at her, momentarily blinded by the spotlight in the ceiling above her head, and offered her kneecap the boot.

'Would you like me to…'

'Yes…yes…'

He looked down. Gently tugged and eased her damp foot into the implausibly inflexible boot. Was she sure she was a 6? He felt a tap on his shoulder from above. Not the brush of an angel's wing.

There was the briefest pause.

'Look, I know this is stupid… but you know… you should take it as a compliment… you don't half… look at me, would you, you didn't used to be in a band called the Milltown Brothers, did you?'

Matthew paused for a few seconds, labouring with the boot. *'Me in the Milltown Brothers?'* He looked up. *'I think I still am.'*

Fabric

The band slipped painfully away over the year or so following that first Kingsize Screamer gig.

A handful of gigs as Kingsize Screamer, two as Junkie. One or two as a wretched version of the Milltown Brothers, no longer a practical, cohesive entity.

Barney leaving was one thing; they believed they could continue as a four-piece. But 'asking' Nian to leave the band because he had a job was another altogether. Simon tells the story. *'We no longer felt he was fully committed just because he was very happy working as well as doing the band, while we were wallowing in misery. It was frustrating when he couldn't make rehearsals being away somewhere; they were the highlight of our week and showed we were still trying, almost justified our existence. For some weird reason we decided James was the person to explain the situation to Nian, he's hardly your typical hatchet man. And Matthew, who Nian usually shared a room with and who is very much the leader, should have been been the one to do it, but James did it in the pub when all our girlfriends and wives were there too. Not nice, but Nian was really cool about it.'*

This left them with a vacancy. They briefly filled it with Stephen Irvine, former drummer of Lloyd Cole and the

Commotions. Great drummer, but not Nian. They put it down to that old chestnut, perspective. And being compared to where they'd been.

The end beckoned.

A particularly salutary experience came at Kent University in Canterbury. Late 1995. The last men standing, appropriately the Nelson brothers; James had dropped away with a job, other musical options and his new girlfriend, Kathy. Simon and Matthew ended up as the Milltown Brothers with someone James knew on bass and his dad on drums. If it sounds desperate, the reality was worse. Matthew is convinced the father and son were playing a different song to the one they thought they were playing throughout the set and sometimes playing a different song to one another. It really was time to find something else to do.

Yet here's the thing. As five became a mixed bag of fast and slow fresh starts, and stops and starts, forward steps and backward steps, the Milltown Brothers as an entity still existed. Besides which, they never managed to fall out; quite the opposite. Nian even went to see the band without him in it within a few months of being sacked. And enjoyed it. They all went off and did their things with varying degrees of relief, detachment, regret, baggage, tears and success. But they stayed great friends. With partners. With babies. With children. And this idea that had dominated their lives for so long just hung around, while most of the time they did something else. The band had become such a profound thing in the Nelson family that it continued to define, influence and colour their entirety. And each band member frustratingly realised their children would never know how big, mad and crazy it had been for a while for their dads.

But without any of them making a big deal about it, the Milltown Brothers assumed an amorphous thereness. Part of the fabric of all their lives, like it always had been, causing moments of frustration, anguish and anger for Simon and Matthew. But that was as much about how they were feeling as what the Milltown Brothers weren't doing. And as their perspectives and bodies changed, their relationship to the Milltown Brothers gradually became a little more characterised by the realisation of how lucky they'd been and what great things they'd done.

It may seem ironic. Particularly given how the industry had reacted to their crass, burdened name that shaped everything. Milltown? Huh. This grammar school band who called themselves brothers as if they were some workers' collective?

If the cynics could see them ... 30 years later, getting on with their own something else to do, but still all as brotherly as hell, four of them still living – more or less – where they were born, and now and again still making magic together.

Bones

Time for a few facts. The first Kingsize Screamer gig was the last for both Barney and Nian. One knew it; the other didn't. The band didn't play again until the next Kingsize Screamer gig, almost six months later at the same venue, the Rock Garden on 30 November 1994. In-between Nian was sacked, then attended the second gig as a punter and enjoyed it. James played lead guitar, Simon played bass and Stephen Irvine was on drums. Kingsize Screamer played four more gigs, all in London and the last at the Borderline in April 1995. Then a band called Junkie, featuring the same line up as Kingsize Screamer, played two gigs in London towards the end of 1995 before the Milltown Brothers' Canterbury humiliation. There was to be a *Best Of* album, 30 or so gigs and another name change before a return to the Milltown Brothers and their third album arrived in 2004.

The Best of the Milltown Brothers was released by Spectrum Music in 1997. It was compiled with the aid of a very blunt instrument and used the artwork from *Valve*. At first glance it could be mistaken for *Valve*, but it's the bastard half-brother of *Valve* or something of that nature. Its twelve songs include all the tracks from *Slinky*, plus the first two singles from *Valve*: 'Turn Off' and 'It's All Over Now, Baby Blue'.

The sleeve notes are surprisingly informative and entertaining, the description of the origins of the album title *Slinky* echoing my take without mentioning The La's. Only the writer's slight exaggeration of the intensity of Matthew's love of the Byrds, the claim that Big Round Records was the band's own record label and momentarily confusing the north-east with the north-west are arguable. As to the album, its existence came as news to the band.

After the Junkie gigs in late 1995, James gave up. Other music projects, a proper job which started as agency work proofreading at Simmons & Simmons, a city law firm, and girlfriend Kathy would become his wife.

After the Canterbury humiliation, the next gig was to be the first by the Milltown Brothers in two years at the Burnley Mechanics in August 1997. Simon, Matthew and Nian all lived in London and had started meeting up regularly to play together, along with Steve Taylor, a work colleague of Simon's, who replaced James on bass. They were supported by Barney's band, the Cosmos. A couple of months later, the same line-up played a gig at the Borderline in London, mixing old Milltown Brothers songs with new ones written by Matthew and Simon.

Around this time Nian got to know a young lawyer called Ciro Romano, whose partner worked with him and Joely at high-end swimsuit designer Liza Bruce, his next stop after Black Katz. Ciro worked for Universal and was keen to get into band management. As a result, Matthew was invited to his flat to play him some of his new songs, including 'Not Alone', 'Wake Up', 'Swimmers' and 'Hear Me'. Ciro was sufficiently impressed to start managing the band on the side. They did a demo session at Christian Henson's studio in West London, producing 'Not Alone', 'Wake Up', 'Hobo' and 'Revolver'. Ciro reintroduced the band and their new music to record labels and they played a handful of gigs in London and the Queens Hotel in Burnley. Even though the music was well received, the Milltown Brothers were old news, so Ciro suggested changing their name to give the music a chance as they headed into 1999. Timing is everything, it made much more sense than the last time. After all, they really were a different band with different songs.

Milo was born. Nobody has a clue where the name came from. The band went into Christian Henson's studio in 1999 and demoed 'She's So Young', 'Me To You', 'I'll Face It', 'Me Myself' and 'Swimmers'. Both RCA and Island showed interest. The band went into Island Studios and came out with 'You Are Here', 'Hear Me', 'Eraser' and 'Rendition'. 'Swimmers' featured in the film *One More Kiss* (2000), directed by Vadim Jean. The band put together a five-track promotional CD featuring 'She's So Young', 'September Comes Around', 'Swimmers', 'Me To You' and 'Eraser'. They played ten gigs around London, including at the Hope & Anchor and two at the Garage between August 1999 and April 2000. By which time interest had... evaporated. However good the music might be, nobody wanted what now represented second-rate Madchester and Britpop survivors. Milo was dead in the water.

In 2002 the Milltown Brothers reappeared with a one-off gig at Burnley Mechanics, followed by another a year later. Meanwhile Matthew had written an ostensibly optimistic love song called 'Cloud Nine' among a bunch of new songs, the fire was rekindled and the original band, though somewhat scattered, created their third album.

Rubberband

Released on Rubber Band Records in 2004, this was an independent, self-financed – and financially unfortunate – project by the band, supported by Laurence Hoare, creator of the band's first website. It featured a CD of material written and recorded upstairs at the Derby Arms in Colne during 2002 and 2003, with Glenn Skinner producing and elder brother Mark given a co-writing credit on 'Sunday Morning', plus there was a bonus CD of 15 tracks. Three gigs were played in support of *Rubberband*: at the Roadhouse in Manchester, the Borderline in London – which witnessed the second coming of Jesus – and the King Street Bar, Accrington. These were to be their last for six years. There was a session on Nelson local radio featuring 'When

A Heart Stops Bleeding' and 'A Song', and one on Gideon Coe's Radio 6 Music show featuring 'When A Heart Stops Bleeding' and 'Sally Ann'.

> 'Me And You'
> 'Cloud Nine'
> 'Rhyme'
> 'When A Heart Stops Beating'
> 'Goodbye'
> 'Surprise Me'
> 'Wide Open'
> 'December 1994'
> 'A Song'
> 'Sunday Morning'
> 'Everything'

The bonus CD featured material recorded in various guises – including Kingsize Screamer and Milo – between 1989 and 1999 and not previously featured on any Milltown Brothers release.

> 'Inkwell'* (1990)
> 'So What She Said'* (1989)
> 'Career'* (1994)
> 'Freeze Frame'* (1993)
> 'Central Reservation'^ (1994)
> 'A Lot Like Love'^ (1994)
> 'Outskirts Of Newmarket'^ (1994)
> 'On Our Street'* (1995)
> 'Not Alone'** (1998)
> 'Wake Up'** (1998)
> 'Swimmers'** (1999)
> 'Here With Me'** (1999)
> 'Hear Me'** (1999)
> 'Eraser'** (1999)
> 'Rendition'** (1999)
> *Milltown Brothers ^Kingsize Screamer **Milo

Jonathan Bibby

Now is the time to introduce Jonathan Bibby, who has already been mentioned on a number of occasions. From this point in the story Jonathan begins to be actively involved in the band's activities, ultimately becoming archivist, unpaid manager, booker and fixer. The gig list at the end of this book, origination of rarities CDs, production of new CDs, merchandise and band's gigs in the past 20 years have all involved him. The support and help he has given to the Milltown Brothers, and the enthusiasm, knowledge and resources he's contributed to this book, are beyond valuable. He has another job that pays the bills.

When he was 16, he was in the audience at the sold-out Burnley Mechanics gig of Barney's first band, Plastic Spearmen. A couple of years later he noticed Barney had joined another band calling themselves the Milltown Brothers, whose track 'Janice Is Gone' he thought one of the highlights of the now mythical 1988 *Manchester, North of England* compilation cassette.

In April 1989 buying the Milltown Brothers' first independent release, *Coming From The Mill*, followed by seeing them live at the Boardwalk in Manchester – the first of well over 60 of their gigs he's attended – sealed his love for the band. He's an avid gig-goer and record collector – not just of the Milltown Brothers – and thinks he owns every song they've demoed, on all manner of formats. All bar the forgotten 'Tomorrow', that is. He also has a huge collection of band ephemera.

Having never clapped eyes on one another before I started this book, we've laughed, cried and moaned in harmony several times in the last 16 months or so.

More *Valve*

Very little – nothing in the public domain – happened between 2004 and 2007, but at the beginning of 2007 an Apple-only digital album gathering up B-sides and 'lost songs' never previously released on album quietly got the ball rolling. This was the work of Jonathan.

At first sight, you may think this album is the ghostly bastard half-brother of the bastard half- brother *Best of*. But it's better than that; it's the partner release to *More Slinky*, the Japan-only release from 1991 on A&M. An almost silk purse that looks slightly like a pig's ear, with its faded, green hued version of the *Valve* cover, reminiscent of pop artist Jasper John's American flags in its own ragged, frankly magnificent way. Accidental or not, it's my personal favourite Milltown Brothers album cover art by some distance. It makes more sense and is much more impactful than the *Valve* original.

As with *More Slinky*, the track listing is long and lovely. Another gathering of maligned choice tracks that astonishingly didn't make the cut. (Although 'Freedom Song' is not good, at least not good enough.) It also includes the Bob Dylan covers that the band were asked in that non-negotiable way to record to support 'It's All Over Now, Baby Blue'. To illustrate the lost potential gathered here, let's take just one song as an example, 'Rosemary Page'. As recently as December 2024 a fan lamented on Facebook: *'I'll never understand why such a glorious track was never a single and only a B-side to be honest'*. This was a song that as far back as October 1991 was identified as a likely follow-up to the rerelease of 'Apple Green' by Debbie Murrell in her first issue editing the fanzine *Coming From The Mill*. It didn't even make it on to *Valve*.

'Worldwide'
'Sleepwalking' (re-recorded version)
'Freedom Song'
'Caroline'
'Sweet Nothing'
'Alice'
'Rosemary Page'
'Can't Find the Time'
'Got This Feeling'

'Long Time'
'Fee Fie Foe Fum'
'Everybody Knows'
'You Don't Know Me No More'
'Positively 4th Street'
'I Shall Be Released'
'Hurricane'

The origins of all these tracks have already been described in Part 4, but enough of dwelling on past glories. Or maybe not. Because the Milltown Brothers *The Best of Expanded Edition* was released by Cherry Red in June 2009.

As with the 1997 version it includes all ten tracks from *Slinky* and the first two singles from *Valve*, and 'It's All Over Now, Baby Blue'. And to justify the phrase *'expanded edition'* adds:

'Sleepwalking' (third and final single from *Valve*)
'Apple Green' (single remix)
'Sally Ann' (acoustic)
'Nationality' (demo)
'Something Cheap' (demo – which to this day Simon prefers to the album version)

There's not much in the way of deeply considered selections here. I'm sorry, 'Sandman' is not a better song than 'Falling Straight Down' or 'Don't Breathe In'. Worse still – and difficult as it is to believe – it gives us cover art to rival *Valve* in its mediocrity. A pinky-red line sketch on a white background of the band's faces, appearing even closer to the womb than the age they were when the band formed almost 22 years earlier in December 1987.

The sales notes accompanying the album shower the band with praise and platitudes. Describing the tracks as being *'tweaked and mastered for the modern age'*, they finish with a prescient flourish. *'In the heat of the late 80s UK scene, many bands came and went, leaving no trace but a single memorable song (if they were lucky). Milltown Brothers however, rose above the pack*

and, although they may not have reached the heady heights achieved by some of their contemporaries, left behind them an enjoyable catalogue scattered with a handful of hits and timely anthems... the Milltown Brothers still find themselves in high regard, and are occasionally active with live shows and online activity.'

A year later in 2010 the band sidled back into the local spotlight by dominating the roster at the And Finally... Festival at the Muni, Colne which offered *'the chance to wallow in a bit of nostalgia'* and was organised by Mark Nelson among others. Seven of the bands on the bill featured members of the Milltown Brothers.

Long Road

Almost three years passed after the And Finally... Festival before the Milltown Brothers played again, and it was again at the Muni, Colne in November 2012. Then another two and a half years before they played the Fan Zone at Turf Moor for Burnley's game against Leicester City in the Premier League on 25 April

2015. Burnley were in danger of relegation from the Premier League, which they'd reached in 2009. They dominated the game yet managed to lose 1-0, which made the difference between survival and relegation.

The impact of the wretched fortune the Milltown Brothers believed they brought with them to the game is best left to Burnley's manager Sean Dyche, a man not prone to flights of fancy. *'The game is cruel sometimes. I think that was a show of it today when it was at its cruellest. Their keeper, arguably their man of the match, has made big saves for them. We miss a penalty and they score 60 seconds later...'*

At the time, the Milltown Brothers had regathered as a unit a few months earlier and were in the process of recording and mixing their first new album for 11 years e. A month later the band played a gig at Manchester Academy as part of the Gigantic Indie All Dayer, alongside Echo & the Bunnymen, Inspiral Carpets and the High.

The band's fourth album was released three months later, on 31 July 2015. Perhaps it's best to print the entirety of the surprising review – surprising in that it was even reviewed – by Paul Scott-Bates on louderthanwar.com. In just over 200 words – before he begins eulogising about the specific tracks on the album – he summarises a good half of this book. And I can happily forgive him that he thought it was the band's first new album for 25 years. I hope he'll forgive me the bold highlight a third of the way through his words.

'**31 July 2015**
8.5 / 10
Lancashire Indie quintet return with their fourth album. *Louder Than War*'s Paul Scott-Bates reviews.

Perhaps it's because The Milltown Brothers come from Lancashire.
Perhaps they evoke memories of seeing them play live at Burnley Mechanics Theatre on their Slinky tour.

*Perhaps standing on the terraces at Turf Moor knowing they
may well be watching Burnley play too.*

*Perhaps it's being asked at one of their gigs the origins of a
psychedelic BFC t-shirt.*

*Perhaps it's the pride of seeing a band from the next town
being touted by* NME *as the next big thing.*

*Perhaps it's seeing Which Way Should I Jump creep inside the
Top 40 singles.*

*Perhaps it's the glow created when they contributed the theme
to the BBC's* Preston Front *drama.*

**Perhaps it could all have been different had some
dodgy dealings by A&M Records not stopped 'Here I
Stand' going Top 10.**

*Perhaps it's the fact that all five members are back again for
their first album in 25 years.*

*Perhaps it's because they were once supported by a little group
called Oasis.*

*Perhaps it's because they were one of the finest jangly Indie
guitar bands around at the time.*

*Perhaps many a Lancashire lad wanted to be in The
Milltown Brothers.*

*Perhaps it's their ability to still record brilliant, infectious
tunes like they've never been away.*

*Perhaps it's because Long Road will grow and grow on you
with each and every listen.*

*Perhaps it's because the title track and new single is an
absolute belter.*

*Perhaps Rockville is one of their finest tunes, with a chorus
that sends goosebumps down your arms.*

*Perhaps the involvement of producers Mark Jones and Mark
Phythian (Coldplay, but don't let that put you off) shows
the confidence of the 11 tracks on board.*

*Perhaps Hideaway – with surely one of the longest lines in
a song ever – is a hark back to the classic Indie era of the
early 90s.*

Perhaps Long Road is an album that could see the Milltown Brothers repeat their huge success in Europe and Japan.

Perhaps the hordes of fans that adored them a quarter of a century ago will re-appear and lovingly clutch this album to their chests.

Perhaps Portrait has a fab guitar riff that sees it as one of the many highlights of the album.

Perhaps Boy Kisses The Girl is just a cavalcade of fab guitars and catchy melodies.

Perhaps you can imagine banks of ecstatic 40-something's jumping around to the rocky beat of Part Of Me.

Perhaps Alive is a gorgeous and fitting end to a surprisingly good album.

Perhaps The Milltown Brothers have just released one of the most perfect guitar-led, Indie albums of the year.'

There's little more to be said. Other than 'Portrait' is the final part of the trinity that is my three favourite Milltown Brothers songs. And Matthew wrote them all.

With the help of Jonathan they released *Long Road* themselves, did very little to promote it and it sold a few hundred CD copies – all that were produced. There was a session on Radio Lancashire in September when 'Here I Stand', 'Rockville', 'Sally Ann' and 'Long Road' were played. And one more gig was played at the Shiine On Weekender at Butlin's Minehead in November. Barney couldn't make it and Christian Madden, Liam Gallagher's keyboard player, deputised. Christian is a great player, but he's not Barney. The front and back artwork explains the rest, including that the band were augmented on pedal steel by Gary Thistlethwaite.

Stockholm

The Milltown Brothers' fifth album *Stockholm* was released on CD four-and-a-half years later, on 1 June 2020. Other than the recording of the album, little had happened in the meantime.

Nothing happened after its release. No gigs. No promotion. Nothing. Once again, the album sold out the few hundred copies that Jonathan Bibby produced.

The cover – and the CD itself – has probably the least detail of any album I've seen that isn't deliberately minimalist, and there is no insert either. You get the album title, band name, a painting of Stockholm on the front and the eight songs listed on the back. That's it.

But I can tell you that Matthew once again wrote all the songs and James produced and mixed it in his home studio. 'Stockholm', the opening track, is similarly paced and musically – if not lyrically – aligned with 'Long Road'. The painting on the cover, signed by J.W. Kelly is a digital image of Stockholm created by Gary Noden, a big fan of the band. It depicts the story behind the song 'Stockholm', the figures in the bottom right foreground being Matthew holding hands with a girl and the other three band members trailing along behind (Barney having shot off ahead and out of frame). The ginger blonde hair of the Nelson brothers is a striking part of the composition.

The third track, with the vibe of a late '60s Californian hippy commune, is a reworking of 'Rainbow Woods', a demo from 1992 that was plucked from obscurity by Jonathan. 'F.I.L.A.', another single taken from the album, proved a hit with the audience when the band next played live, over three years later.

Tongue-Tied Mesmerised

By far the most interesting of the Milltown Brothers compilation albums was released in 2022 and featured all the tracks from their independent singles, with the not quite independent 'Seems To Me' and a series of demos from 1987 to 1990, including the EMI demo of 'Which Way Should I Jump?' as well as the version recorded at Strawberry Studios which was released as their second single. Jonathan was once again responsible.

Simply, sparsely but neatly packaged, the album has a photograph of the band on the front taken at the same time by

Tim Paton as the one that appears on the back of the *Coming From The Mill* 12" single from 1989. The tracks on the album demonstrate what a potent band the Milltown Brothers were in the good two years it took Tim to get them signed by A&M. The lovely title of the album was lifted from the lyrics of 'Which Way Should I Jump?' and describes how Matthew and Simon felt about speaking with potential record labels when they were desperate to get signed.

The next gig that took place was in August 2023 when the band surprised themselves by playing a sold-out show at the Trades Club, Hebden Bridge, then sold out the Kanteena in Lancaster on 25 November, Barnoldswick Arts Centre on 23 December, and six months later St Mary's Chamber in Rawtenstall on 3 May 2024. Having attended the last two of these gigs, I can assure you they were ecstatic and memorable.

Part 6
BREATHING (1994–2025)

This Part of the book gives each member of the band the freedom to say whatever they like and how they feel about it all and one another. Let's start with Barney.

Barney

"I had become increasingly disillusioned with the Milltown Brothers throughout the second album. Not with the lads, or even with the music really, but things seemed to be starting to gradually become unhinged in more ways than one. As I remember, there was a shake-up at the record company and we were dealing with different people, people who had not been involved in signing us or helping us create the first album. It started to feel that they were honouring the second album more because of contractual obligations than because they wanted to. Like the money they must have been down wasn't their fault, so they could give us a hard time, we weren't their responsibility. I'm sure they had their own favourites on the label; I recall demos being rejected almost instantly because they weren't like *Slinky* songs and got the feeling they wanted us to make *Slinky 2* and wouldn't let the band develop in the way it was naturally doing. I was caught unawares when A&M offered us John Reid as manager, and I got that wrong, but I didn't trust A&M's motives – which, looking back, was not clever.

Once I'd made the decision to leave, I focused all my attention on what I wanted to do, which was music, albeit a different path. Well, I say that, but after telling the guys straight after the Derby show, I'm told I finished the tour and in 1994 did *Pebble Mill*, the Holland dates, Morecambe and the first Kingsize

158

Screamer gig. I don't have much memory of this, but as I hated the last of these I must have been there, but it was over, I was out despite my love for them.

I'd been studying jazz piano again with Patricia Schofield for a while and restarted classical lessons with Mr Sutcliffe, the guy who first tried to teach me all those years ago. I did this to improve my technique and further my knowledge. The Associated Board of the Royal Schools of Music (ABRSM) practical instrumental grades range from 1 to 8. Mr Sutcliffe decided I should work towards grade 5, which I did. I took the exam and passed with distinction. Patricia had studied at Leeds College of Music, one of England's music conservatoires, now called Leeds Conservatoire, on the jazz course and this was what I wanted to do. I applied and got an audition. After my audition, I was told all degree students must be grade 8 level, in both practical and theory, but was offered their year-long access course starting in the autumn of 1994. If I passed and achieved my grade 8 at the same time, I could re-audition for the BA Hons in Jazz Studies, so that's what I did and I finally graduated in the summer of 1998 with a 2:1. The third of the Milltown Brothers to get a degree – wonders will never cease.

I loved it at Leeds. I didn't move there, I commuted on the train for four years. I had a few part-time jobs in Burnley while I was doing it. One of them was at Our Price record shop and I'm told it was me that came across a Milltown Brothers *Best of* CD when I was unpacking some deliveries and none of the band knew it existed. I can't remember any of this, but it says it all that not only were we not consulted, they couldn't be bothered to tell us they were releasing it. But what did it matter? I honestly never thought I'd be playing any of those songs again. As for not moving to Leeds, I had no desire to live the party student life; I'd done all that and then some with the band. I just wanted to learn as much as I could from some amazing tutors who also worked in the industry. I must have been a great student.

My instrumental teacher in my first year was Manchester's finest, Joe Palin (RIP). Joe was a bebop pianist, extremely well respected. He didn't like travelling, so his name perhaps didn't reach as far as it could have, but he had played with some of the biggest names when they came to Manchester, as he was the house pianist at Club 43, a legendary Manchester jazz club in the 1950s and 60s. Among many others Joe had worked as a sideman for Zoot Sims, Art Farmer, Ronnie Scott and Tubby Hayes, all big, big names. Although it was wonderful to learn from Joe, he was in his sixties when I met him, and I think it's fair to say, hadn't looked after himself very well and as a result, was often absent or in the bar.

For my second two years, the internationally renowned Nikki Iles was my tutor. Nikki is a brilliant pianist, composer and bandleader and she continues to tour the world doing all three. I have never wanted to be an out-and-out jazz musician but had a strong desire to learn everything I could about how it all works. In that regard, the Leeds Conservatoire was brilliant.

A few years before – in August 1992, I'm told – in our on-going quest to please A&M, the Milltown Brothers had been working on some demos in a studio in Burnley. It was owned by Michael Handley above his TV aerial business. The engineer on the session was his son, 16-year-old Danny, who I christened Handlebars for no reason other than the obvious. Although he was a good few years younger than me, we shared a love of the blues and became good friends. He could sing and was both talented on the guitar and knowledgable about music far beyond his years and we started doing a few gigs together which culminated in the Cosmos, the band I started playing in after leaving the Milltown Brothers. It was a great band and allowed me to venture into more jazz and funk-inspired music. I suppose it was akin to the acid jazz style that was happening in the 1990s. We ended up supporting Kingsize Screamer at a local gig in Nelson at the Good Night Club – a few years later, I had my wedding do there! Much as I hate to say it, we went down extremely well with the audience, who were very familiar with the Milltown Brothers, but it didn't work for Kingsize Screamer. I remember feeling my decision to leave had been fully vindicated.

Around the time, I met and fell in love with a girl called Liza. My long relationship and engagement to Julie – sister of Stephen Rigg, a hardcore Milltown Brothers fan who I met quite a few years earlier at a Plastic Spearmen gig – was over. My relationship with Liza was often fiery, a little like a roller coaster at times with many ups and downs. However, we are still together 30 years later. We have two wonderful children: Dexter Jay Williams, who is now producing house music, DJing all over the place and generating millions of hits on SoundCloud, he's already released some music on Polydor too; and Macy May Williams, who has a fantastic voice and we are starting to perform together, which is a dream come true. They make me proud every day, are talented and hard-working and my best friends. Neither of them seems to have any intention of moving out of the family home, and I wouldn't have it any other way.

I was with the Cosmos for a couple of years, after which I left, mainly due to some personal problems I was having at the time. But while still studying at Leeds I'd started another band with a group of friends at home who'd been involved with local outfits and done well. Bruce had been the singer with Beware the Green Monkey, who played with the Milltowns quite a few times, Chris Hartley on guitar, Chris Precious drums and Nick on bass. We called ourselves the Rubbish as a joke and it wasn't meant to be a serious venture, it was a reason to get together every week, have a few beers and make some music. It was a bit similar to how things had been with the Milltown Brothers in the early days. We wrote some silly songs, which turned out to be pretty good. So we recorded an album called *Crazy Farmers* with the wonderful Mark Jones, despite him being a Blackburn fan (which took some getting over).

'This has got to be the most goddamned happy, uplifting album ever! Shame the lads don't have worldwide fame and recognition for their clever and funny work.' Unpopular1. rate your music.com. July 2002

Mark has a recording studio, MJM, in Oswaldtwistle, and has worked with countless local and not so local artists including the likes of Space, Black Grape, Peter Gabriel *and...* us, the Milltown Brothers. We recorded *Long Road* with him 16 years after the Rubbish had a lot of fun doing *Crazy Farmers* in a week during 1998. He is a fantastic engineer/producer, musician and a good friend. One of our songs was used as a jingle on Radio 1, the Kevin Greening show, and we supported Status Quo at several gigs, including two at Wembley Arena in 1999. We eventually changed our name to Tidy because the people who were promoting us were sick of pushing water uphill. The whole thing fizzled out a couple of years later, but amazingly we were asked to play at Kendal Calling in 2018 to mark the 20th anniversary of *Crazy Farmers*. We did it with just a few hours practice..

While my children were young I had ten years, 1999 to 2009, teaching music at Nelson and Colne College – where my life was transformed by Adrian Douthwaite's 12-bar blues piano – plus doing private piano lessons and being in local function bands – Soul combo Superfly with wayward Ben being the best. If you went out with Ben, you came home with a beard; it's good for my well-being he now lives in Oxfordshire.

Around this time *Q* magazine had a regular feature on bands that hadn't been seen for a while called 'Where Are They Now?'. They did it on the Milltowns and I remember joking with Matt when it came out that all that was left now was the identity parade on *Never Mind the Buzzcocks*, where they pick out a person who was originally in an old band who'd had some success. Sometime later and, lo and behold, Matt rang me to say they wanted me to do it. I'm quite sure what that meant was no one else in the band was prepared to do it, so muggins got the job. My initial response was a firm no, but when Matt pointed out the BBC would pay for Liza and I to travel down on the train, pick us up from the station and put us up in a 4-star hotel, I became slightly more interested. He went on to say I would be paid £350 for my troubles. I was in. We arrived at Euston and were whisked to White City in a black Mercedes, put in a dressing room and informed they were filming, but my segment wouldn't be *'until about nine o'clock'*. It was only five. As luck would have it, a young trainee/

work experience lad knocked on the door shortly afterwards and asked if we'd like anything to drink. Yes indeed. *'I would like a strong continental lager and the missus would like a glass of Shiraz, please. And could you please bring the same every 20 minutes?'*

'No problem,' said the lad, who coincidentally was from Colne. I can't remember his name, although I wish I could. Shortly after the first instalment of booze arrived, so did Loz – Laurence Hoare, a friend of the band who'd put together our first website and did some stuff for us on *Rubberband*. He was laden with exotic herbs and spices.

By the time we filmed my bit, all was good. The only panel members I knew were Bill Bailey, a great piano player, although I didn't know at the time, and Sam Brown. A few years before I was in a car with Fraz and I heard Sam Brown's 'Stop!' on the radio. I had never heard or seen her before but proclaimed my love for her right there and then. After smoking some weed with Number 2 in the identity parade – I think I was 4 – we went to the green room and I started chatting with Ms Brown, having a laugh and all was good. I think I was correctly picked out. A jolly good day out was had by all... other than when compère Mark Lamarr arrived in the green room, someone who'd always come across to me as a good guy. Without a word he bluntly interrupted my conversation with Sam and turned his back on me. It's something and nothing, but that kind of thing isn't nice and I hope it was a one-off.

Thankfully, I was made redundant from college when they closed the music department. I say thankfully purely for personal reasons, as firstly it made me return to playing full-time, and secondly it meant I didn't have to be a teacher anymore, something that always made me feel like a charlatan. It was a real shame they shut the music department down, though – austerity measures – as it was great and well respected, but, aside from the odd piano lesson, I'm not cut out to be a teacher.

During this time I was aware Matthew and Simon had started writing some songs and were getting together to play whenever they could. Then they started talking about doing a new album that became *Rubberband*. To be honest, I wasn't overly excited. For me the band was done as a thing. As brilliant as it was and however amazing it could have been if things had gone slightly differently, it was over. Not that I wasn't proud of what we achieved. I was, very. Not that I didn't enjoy the ride, I did, big time. Not that I hadn't made brilliant friends for life, I had. But that was then and this was now. I didn't get too involved, but did play keys on it. And that was that... or so I thought.

I worked for a time with Fraz writing theme tunes and jingles for adverts while I was still teaching, Matthew having got us a foot in the door at Granada Television where he'd ended up working. Not only is Fraz a great musician, he is also a hairy dogman and a great friend. We roomed together around the world with the band and I can honestly say I don't think any two other human beings have talked as much utter nonsense bullshit as us. Hilarious. We also wrote a song called 'Pusherman' for Simon Webbe from Blue when he went solo; it appeared as a hidden track on his debut solo album in 2005 and paid for an all-inclusive family holiday in Ibiza!

After the teaching I spent 11 years with Barry Steele & Friends, a rock 'n' roll theatre show where I played in the backing band and also did a couple of sets each night bashing out Jerry Lee Lewis songs, which was great. We played at theatres all over the UK. Much to the disgust of Alan 'The Hat' Whitham, who plays bass (very well) and with whom I travelled and became and remain good friends, I can't remember the names of many of the theatres where we played, but I do remember playing at the Adelphi in the West End and the Olympia in Dublin – oh and the Benidorm Palace. I did well over a thousand gigs with the show all over the UK, Europe and Scandinavia. To have such a massive number of gigs guaranteed while the kids were growing up was a godsend and much appreciated.

In the middle of all this, around 10 years after *Rubberband*, Matthew started writing songs seriously again and this time was keen to get the band back together. I think life passing by with his children growing up had prompted him, and *Long Road* was the starting point. The theatre gigs were great but different from a band, and I had some down time between tours. Also I think enough time had passed, the sound of Kingsize Screamer had faded from my lugholes, and so when the Milltown Brothers stirred again I started to enjoy being more involved in the process of the next two albums, *Long Road* and *Stockholm*. 'Long Road' is one of my favourite Milltown songs and I really enjoyed the different musical avenues we explored even though because of various commitments – usually mine – we didn't manage many live shows.

Meanwhile Danny Handlebars had moved on and up and had been travelling the world, playing and singing with John Steel's Animals and Friends. John was the original drummer with the Animals and had been touring with this latest version of the band since the early 1990s when it was started with Hilton Valentine (RIP), the band's original guitarist, and Dave Rowberry (RIP), the keyboard player who joined when Alan Price left in the 1960s. I'd actually been asked to join the band in 2003 when Dave died; I remember being keen to join as I loved the Animals, Alan Price being a big influence on me as a youngster, but it never came off for one reason or another.

What actually happened was Micky Gallagher joined. Micky had played with the band briefly in the 1960s, was the Blockheads' keyboard player and played on two Clash albums. Fast-forward to 2020, Micky refused to be vaccinated for Covid, wasn't allowed to travel, and subsequently – with a nudge from Handlebars, I'm sure – I got the call. Finally I was an Animal. Big news for me. Not only do I get to travel around the world playing rhythm and blues, I get to do it with Handlebars, my good old friend. I love listening to John's stories from the 1960s too. Not only was he a founding member of the Animals, but when the band ended, he worked for his mate Chas Chandler (the original Animals bass player) who had moved into band management. Chas was responsible for bringing Jimi Hendrix to London and managing him, and looked after the mighty Slade when they were all over the charts in the early 1970s.

Which brings us more or less up to date. We – the Milltowns – played another handful of gigs in 2023, which I think we all really enjoyed and the result was we decided to make another album, which is happening as I write. It's going to be a corker and I have loved the way we've recorded it, as much as possible live, together in the studio. We've done it at Chris Lewis's Groove Studio in Burnley. Chris is doing a cracking job, even though things seem to be taking much longer to mix than it took to record. I also loved the handful of gigs we did in 2024: seeing old faces and meeting up with people I haven't seen for years makes me happy. Nobby, our brilliant sound engineer from the 'glory' days, has taken time off from his huge bands and global tours to be front of house in the Lexington on Pentonville Road, and again at the brilliant 100 Club on Oxford Street in 2025. You can't help but notice him. He's as tall as a lamp post.

In the 1990s I don't think I fully appreciated how good the Milltown Brothers were and still are. I was so young with hardly anything to compare it to, and while I loved it, they were into different music to me. Simon didn't play like B.B. King, Nian listened to Bob Dylan. They all listened to Neil Young and REM. As it turns out, it's great that Simon doesn't play like B.B. King, he plays like Simon Nelson, and no one else does. He is very dynamic, extremely melodic, he believes in every note he plays. And so he should. Nian is a machine, one of the most solid drummers I've ever played with – but when you're 18 and have only played with a couple of drummers, you don't realise. When you're 55 and have played with scores of them, you do. His dynamics drive the band. You know all about my feelings for Fraz both as a musician and a person, and Matthew continuously takes me through every emotion with his lyrics, and every couple of weeks he takes me to the pub too. He's a very good man, he went through hell for years when the band lost its way, but it's never changed a thing about what we think about each other. And still it seems this thing that was done for me by 1994 rolls on over 30 years later.'

Nian

'14 October 1993. I always made the effort to go and see support bands play, and tonight was no different. They were very good. Powerful and melodic. The only issues were the drummer wasn't great and the singer had a great voice and undeniable presence but seemed to be mimicking Ian Brown from the Stone Roses in his stagecraft and in my head that ship had sailed a few years previously.

I ended up watching the whole show and as they launched into the Beatles' 'I Am The Walrus' to finish, was convinced that if they could nail the middle eight of this particular song – '*sitting in an English garden waiting for the sun, if the sun don't come you get a tan from standing in the English rain...*' – then they were a band to be reckoned with. Nail it, they did. As they left the stage and made their way back to the dressing room, Jonathan Bibby leaned into me and said, '*It's over.*' I didn't have a clue what he was talking about, but when I asked him about it years later he said he just thought the moment struck him, with our loss of spark and the spark and buzz this unknown band created... a good portion of the crowd were there for them. I made a point of telling the lead guitarist how good I thought they were, which was acknowledged with a '*Thanks, mate*' and a look of 'You don't need to tell me how good we are.'

Fast-forward two and half years; I'm standing in a field with family and friends, along with 120,000 others at one of two shows at Knebworth, that apparently half the country had applied for tickets to see...and it's the same band headlining. Evidently, the singer's circa 1989 Mancunian posturing worked for him.

Oasis's support at Knebworth came from Cast and the Charlatans. Cast fronted by John Power from The La's had played what I think was only their second ever gig supporting us at Colne Municipal Hall around 1992 – which came about from us having toured with The La's. The Charlatans we had toured with in March/April '92. The whole Knebworth weekend in some ways was the coronation of the Britpop movement...which of course, did not involve us.

167

In hindsight, we'd given up too soon. Blur had kept at it and were one half of the Blur/Oasis rivalry which gripped the nation... funny. If we'd hung in there for a year or two, the bands influenced by artists from our era were having their day. It's well known Noel Gallagher had been a roadie for Inspiral Carpets; him and Tom Higley nipped into our dressing room to say hello when we supported The La's at Liverpool Royal Court, and with his *'Magpie Eyes... Hungry For The Prize'* had been absorbing and cherry-picking chord progressions, guitar licks and lyrics all along the way. And why wouldn't he? That's how it works.

In 2004 Oasis released a DVD celebrating 10 years since the release of *Definitely Maybe* and someone from the Oasis camp got in touch asking for a Milltown Brother to go and film a talking head for said DVD. I was working in London (and was probably the biggest Oasis fan in the band), so I ended up doing it. I'm there on the DVD having a ramble about the lyrics and chords on 'Live Forever' although it's just the audio and not the actual film of me that made the cut, drummer from the Milltown Brothers not being of significant enough status to be shown on film... which was a fair shout. I think the fact we'd maybe had some small influence on them led to one of us being asked to contribute to the film, but my point being, if we'd hung in there a little longer...

We weren't to know that at the time, and anyway before 1994 the band had become a drag... hard work in a way that creative ventures can be when the natural trajectory is rerouted and things stall. We couldn't get the natural flow back. It had all been so easy in the beginning – our beginning – our collective influences seeped naturally into our output with great results; we didn't need to think about it – Zen like – it just happened. When it doesn't flow and it becomes hard work, the results are never as good and the joy of creating disappears – not through the lack of success, but through a lack of pleasure in the process.

New horizons were popping up everywhere for all of us. I'd met Joely whilst on tour in Japan – a vibrant go-getter of a girl from Atlanta, Georgia, who woke me up from my *chilled-out musician and cosy girlfriend back home* doze. We were 25 years old and had London as a playground. I'd never planned to move to London, I just ended up there.

I got a job letting flats for Black Katz – good people, great fun, a car and for the first time a decent wage coming in, plus a crazy party scene at weekends. Most people working there seemed to be in the same boat – creatives, actors, DJs, club scene casualties, musicians, all having to earn some money to fund their London lifestyle and hopes of getting back into a world of former glory. Working there was good financially, but where were the next adventures coming from?

If I told the younger me I'd spend eight years working in the fashion industry, I'd have thought you were mad – it was so far removed from anything I aspired to. But… Joely had finished her fashion design training at Saint Martins and started work with fashion designer Liza Bruce, whose main business was in the US. I ended up spending time with Liza and her husband Nicholas Alvis Vega, which led to them offering me a job there too. They were an interesting, eccentric, inspiring, slightly out-there couple, somehow keeping a successful fashion label chaotically afloat, and it was obvious travel was going to be a big part of the job; it made sense, and I didn't take much persuading.

It made sense for them too, as they could give me and Joely the business credit card and send us round the world doing press and sales with a new collection twice a year, avoiding expensive agency costs. Hard work and stressful, but the upside: we'd sell the collection and do press appointments from the penthouse at the Royalton Hotel in NYC, Chateau Marmont LA and Marlin Hotel in Miami, where we would stay in the same room for a week in each place… was amazing. Work by day, penthouse living in some of the most fun cities in the US by night. What's not to like as a 25-year-old?

So I was working and travelling more when I started at Liza Bruce, and it became a little more difficult to coordinate rehearsals with the band, and in hindsight it was gradually starting to take a back seat for me. I don't remember it being a huge issue, but I think I was unavailable for a couple of rehearsals on the bounce, we went for a few drinks in Camden, with our wives and girlfriends, and it was James who suggested if I couldn't commit to rehearsals, I should probably leave the band. I don't remember protesting at the time. We were all just coming to terms with the end of the success we'd had, in different ways and at different speeds.

How did I feel? I felt there was an element of them not quite understanding the situation we were in. The band had no money, we were living in London and we had rent to pay, so work was unavoidable. It's just that the job I had meant I had to travel at certain times. Could I have taken a job that meant less travelling? Yes, but I needed to keep moving to stay sane, and sometimes when a door opens you have to walk through it. The band had felt like it was dragging on and on without getting anywhere, and as I'm sure the other lads will agree, it hadn't been a particularly fun place to be, so I think there was an element of relief as well. I remember travelling back to the flat with Joely and thinking, *Well, it's just you and me now.*

At this point the band was something I was extremely proud to have been part of, but it had ended. When you're young, you just keep moving forward, there's a natural momentum that doesn't leave much time for reflection and looking back; I've never particularly liked looking back anyway. Writing this is like pulling teeth. Looking at old photos has always made me feel slightly uneasy too for some reason – better to just keep moving forward – to the next moment...

There would be times when I'd end up in places that I'd previously visited with the band and would really miss them all, just the general humour and camaraderie. I remember going back to the Whiskey a Go Go to watch a band, a venue we'd played on our first US tour, and it brought back all the feelings of when we'd first arrived as a band into LA, so excited and disbelieving at our luck – sitting around the swimming pool on the roof of the Hyatt Hotel on Sunset Strip, all of us wondering how we could make this last. That's the thing with great moments, you know they're going to pass – which is part of what makes them great, I guess. It had felt like such a privilege to have played in iconic venues such as the Whiskey and CBGBs.

I remember a few months after I left I got to see the band play a show at the Rock Garden in Covent Garden. After being part of it for so long, it was like having an out of

body experience, but interesting to see them from the front as opposed to the three rear ends. I remember really enjoying it; they had a good new drummer who'd played with Lloyd Cole and they played a brilliant new song called 'A Lot Like Love' which blew me away, one of the best things they'd done. We all still spent time together, socialising whenever we could, and from what I heard I think I swerved some of the darkest moments.

Fortunately for the lads, humour was a huge part of what made the band as a group of people last – and this never disappeared even when it got desperate. You must have that ability to laugh among yourselves, make each other laugh and more importantly laugh at yourselves and the other worldly situations you find yourself in. Good and bad. The humour was generally self-deprecating, probably as a protective shield against all the ups and downs of band life. In studios, on tour buses, endless hours sitting around in venues and hotels, we could very comfortably be in each other's company for weeks and months on end, and it would be an absolute joy, insane at times, but always fun and that's what you miss the most. Having said that, your close friends are kind of always with you, wherever you are.

Thirty odd years later, whenever we get together, we seem to slip straight back into the same mindset, where making each other laugh is the priority and it's a beautiful thing – a comfortable place to be and something I look forward to as much as making the music.

We were at Liza Bruce for around two years until early 1997, time that included moving to Manhattan to open their US office. We gave notice on our flat in London, the move was meant to be permanent, but the stress involved in working for an artistic/chaotic couple meant our thoughts of starting our own label were expedited. Three months after leaving for the US, we resigned and came back to London; Joely would design and do press, and I would handle production and run the business side of things. We had the contacts, relationships with the press, buyers and manufacturers and ideas on how to improve on the business we'd just been part of. A quick course in business management would fill in the blanks and, after designing the first sample collection, exhibiting it at London Fashion Week and getting some decent orders, I headed out to raise £60,000 to fund production and delivery of the first collection.

In just a few months JoelyNian was a label in its own right. Turns out I really liked running my own business, something I've continued to do in various guises up to the present day.

Matt and Janine, Simon and Rachel and James and Kathy were all in London initially, and I remember Barney coming to stay with me a few times, so we were all still very much in touch. James moved back to the north-west and eventually me, Matt and Simon drifted into playing music together again. Can't be sure on dates, but it must've been around 1998. Steve Taylor, a bass player Simon had met, joined proceedings, and we rehearsed just off Holloway Road once a week. It was great to be back playing drums and having a chilled night with my friends, and the upturn in the outlook of the music reflected this, somehow lighter and with more groove. Steve was so relaxed on bass that he was almost horizontal, but it worked and softened the more earnest tendencies of the three northerners.

A guy called Ciro Romano was married to a girl, Angelina, who also worked at Liza Bruce, so our paths crossed. He was a music lawyer at Universal wanting a shift in direction into music management, so he started taking an interest in the band. He had a go at relaunching the Milltown Brothers but after hitting an industry brick wall we became Milo; RCA and especially Island Records liked some of the songs. The latter paid for us to do some demos and then, well, they didn't fancy damaged goods, besides which the guy that had initially liked the songs lost his job and Milo slipped into the ether. The music industry for unsigned bands in a nutshell. Luck doesn't come close. We had fun and played some shows in and around London. Steve became a dear friend to all of us and was always part of the gang before he passed away far too soon in early 2018. I miss him.

My brother Seth moved to London around 1997 and moved in with me and Joely. We somehow managed to rent a glorious two-bedroom flat in Clifton Hill, St John's Wood, which was way above our station and anything we could possibly afford at the time. It was owned by a prominent and well published economist who just wanted a nice couple to take care of it and therefore didn't ask for anything like the sort of rent that he could achieve for a flat in such an amazing location (the famed Abbey Road Studios being just around the corner). In order to put ourselves in prime position to get it, we neglected to introduce him to Seth, we'd sneak him in later. We got the flat on the premise that we left alone his life's work, located on shelves and under the bed in the second bedroom. Seth moved in once we had the keys. Just to remind me of my lowly place in the cosmic music standings, Alan McGee – owner/founder of Creation Records and the man who signed Oasis – lived directly across the road and I had to watch his comings and goings at the height of Oasis's fame and notoriety on a daily basis. Liam and Patsy Kensit lived just around the corner – all without needing a break on the rent, I'm guessing.

Eight months into the tenancy, the landlord called me and asked if he could pop round to pick up some of his papers for an upcoming talk that he was booked to do. As he said this, I vaguely remembered arriving back to the flat a few months earlier to see Seth emptying lots of black bin liners into the recycling in an attempt to jazz up his room before the visit of a girlfriend. Ouch! We felt terrible. My time among the music glitterati of London ended abruptly... for the second time.

But JoelyNian grew to the point where we were stocked in some pretty good stores around the world: Harrods, Harvey Nichols, Selfridges, Barneys NY, Saks Fifth Avenue, Beams Japan to name a few. I was in a world of fabric fairs, fashion parties and exhibiting at fashion weeks, not my world at all, but there was fun and travelling to be had. Madonna wore our clothes in videos, Jade Jagger became a friend and would model for us, we were regularly featured in *Vogue*, *i-D*, *Harper's Bazaar*, etc.

It had been hard, but we'd made it work and had grown the business over four or five years – then 9/11 changed the course of things, as it did for so many. Mid-production on a holiday season delivery that was 80 per cent going to the US market, planes were grounded, holidays and holiday clothing orders cancelled. The faxes came through the next day and we had to close the business to save further losses. We'd just signed a deal with Debenhams for them to license our name on a collection for two years, so we were lucky and had some income to keep us going, but I was beginning to lose interest. Joely and I had gone our separate ways as a couple a year earlier – we'd grown apart as a result of working together 24/7 for eight years, plus I was dragging my heels on a suggested relocation to the US. I just didn't see myself living there full time. As I approached 32, I was beginning to lean towards a move home.

I loved my time in London, but every time I got to Euston station or the start of the M1, a sense of heading back to the right place would wash over me. As I spent more time back in the north towards the end of 2000, I started spending it with a wonderful girl called Jo, who I'd known and liked for many years, but we were both with other people at the time. By New Year's Eve 2000 going on to 2001, our paths were clear and I made a beeline for her. We fell in love, and after living between Lancaster and London for a year or so, I committed to moving back to Lancaster. Jo would've much preferred a move to London, but that wasn't possible straight away and I was ready for a change in the pace of life and couldn't wait to get back to where the Lake District was only a stone's throw away. I promised I'd make it up to her.

As is the way with these things, as soon as I'd committed to moving back to Lancaster, Ciro offered me a job at his artist management company – Independent Sound Management.

After years in the fashion industry, it was just the sort of role I was looking for back in the music industry. Ciro had been busy, he was managing Tunde from Lighthouse Family and had just taken on a fantastically talented band from Dublin – HAL. I was mainly brought in to work with them. After chatting with Jo, we decided I should do it, so I started commuting down to London on Monday mornings, returning to Lancaster on Thursday/Friday evenings. Not the relaxed return to the north I'd envisaged, but in some ways the best of both worlds.

HAL signed to Rough Trade Records, Heavenly took up their publishing, and they recorded a wonderful debut album, but despite having some great singles it didn't quite happen for them. I thought genius meant guaranteed success – apparently not. HAL not making it had me seriously doubting the music industry as a whole – if a band this good couldn't break through, then I didn't know what could. Nigel's on to something with this luck thing. They were extraordinary.

Jo and I bought our first house in January 2004 in Lancaster and along with Sam, her 10-year-old son, we moved in to start a new chapter in our lives. Finn, our son, was born on 24 November 2004. After the fantastic experiences I was lucky to have in the first 30 odd years of life, moving into our first house and Finn being born were still the best. Wonderful. Indescribable. A third would follow in August 2006, when Jo and I tied the knot in the Lake District, celebrating with our friends and family aboard the Teal steamer on Lake Windermere. Barney's band played, the sun shone, I'd married my soulmate, and the band was briefly back together in one spot, something that I don't think had happened since we'd recorded and released *Rubberband* in 2004.

When Finn was born, I started working for Ciro and various other managers/labels on a more freelance basis, tour managing and working in live music production, so I could spend more time at home. I knew the ropes from regular touring with the Milltown Brothers, and having run a business, running a budget was relatively easy. Jo – a passionate lover of music, probably more than me these days – enjoyed this side of my work, as most tours would involve the summer music festivals, so we had easy access to Glastonbury and the rest most years. We took full advantage, taking Finn and most of my extended family with us! In 2004 I bumped into Noel Gallagher again backstage at Glastonbury and managed to introduce my Dad, already a big Oasis fan, to him; they chatted at length and discussed how they'd both played 'Revolution' by the Beatles at full blast when the Labour Party came back into power in 1997.

Around this time Matthew started his own TV & film production company – Space Digital – which over the years grew and grew; he would regularly bring me in to work as a production manager/line producer, so we'd get to spend quite a bit of time together, travelling, meeting new people and working on interesting jobs/shoots. Quite often with Nigel in his creative director role in a big northern agency – the man behind this book; it really was his idea, not ours. I appreciated that work, but more than that I loved spending time with my old room-mate – doing what we always did – making light of the world and laughing.

Slightly disillusioned with the music industry after the lack of recognition for such a great band as HAL, I decided to leave it behind and fully intended to, but it didn't last long. In 2009 a young band from Morecambe were brought to my attention and two songs into watching them live, I realised I was going to manage them. Seaside Riot became the Heartbreaks and Joe, Matt, Ryan and Deaks – four wonderful people – would become part of life going forward. A publishing deal and record deal were signed, nine singles and two albums released, support tours with Carl Barât, Morrissey and Hurts among others, a hit single 'Delay, Delay', and minor fame in Japan would follow. Had they existed 18 months earlier, we'd probably have been able to retire on the proceeds – but alas, and again despite undeniable talent, timing or lack of it was all.

The Heartbreaks was a four-year project I was completely immersed in. While undeniably fun and it did pay me a decent wage, I was beginning to grapple with the realisation that no matter how talented the artist and no matter how hard I worked

– the end result and success of it all was in the hands of others. A hangover, the flippant dismissal of a band's single in a playlist meeting at Radio 1 or a random decision over a pint at the *NME* could leave years of work with no route to the top.

With this in mind, and no pension in the pipeline from the music business, aged 45, I decided to put my skills into something that had a more predictable outcome. Working in property at Black Katz all those years ago had planted a seed – a knowledge of property might be useful one day. When Jo and I had bought our house in 2004, we'd kept Jo's old house to rent out, we had some equity in there and that's what we used to get going. It worked. I'm still doing it and I'm my own boss and my time is my own now.

Managing HAL and the Heartbreaks was like buying a lottery ticket. I enjoyed going to sleep at night, wondering 'what if', but ultimately, as with the Milltown Brothers, as with JoelyNian, it was about taking the interesting route in life, Kerouac-like going towards the adventures, the interesting people. We're not here long, so why wouldn't you?

Which leads me nicely to the two albums we've made while I've been making a living through property. *Long Road* happened pretty early on. I was busy, but my time was my own and I like an adventure… one of the great things about the band was it sent us to places we might otherwise not have seen. Osaka, Minneapolis, Aberystwyth, Dusseldorf, Ipswich. Padul was one such place. A small town in the province of Granada in Spain that I think James had visited… and had met a man with a studio. Why Padul? Why not? I can never quite remember how these things come about, but there we found ourselves for five days recording the backing tracks to a new batch of songs that we'd loosely rehearsed, the obvious standout being 'Long Road'.

We recorded during the day and headed to the local bar in the evening for beers, laughs and tapas. One tapas dish being egg and chips. You can eat as much and as badly as you want when it's labelled tapas. Perfect. It's always fun being back together, although our in-house court jester Barney didn't make the Padul trip, and I always look forward to playing music again.

I remember waking up, going for a run down streets that had the snow-capped peaks of the Sierra Nevada at their end, then into the studio to record. A nice existence for a week. We've been very lucky like that. Imagine spending a whole summer in Bath with your best friends, the record company has rented a cool flat for you and you're recording your debut album – which you know is pretty good. That has to be one of the best memories I have of being in the band. We'd amble down the hill to Bath Moles Studio in the morning, it was always sunny, record all day, head out for a couple of drinks, then into the Moles venue to watch a band… and repeat.

James and Barney are always involved in playing music, it's their life. James has his own studio, where he'll spend every spare moment, and if Barney isn't playing piano for pleasure at home, he's at a show playing; both can't exist without playing. Simon and Matthew are constantly writing at home on their guitars, but I on the other hand don't play my drums when I'm not with the band. It's not the sort of instrument you pick up in the living room whilst watching a film, so I have long dormant periods as a player. I play my acoustic guitar for fun, but apart from that, it's a case of trying to pick up where I left off, usually taking a couple of rehearsals to get back into the swing of things. But we all slot back together very well, even after five years of not doing it. We instinctively know how each of the others play, and that is the very fabric of the band.

We recorded some decent backing tracks in Padul and they went off to a man – Mark Jones – with a plan back in Lancashire, to be finished off; vocals, extra guitars, backing vocals etc., then mixing. A lack of budget generally means this process takes too long and the initial momentum can be lost, but we came away with a decent batch of songs and an album. The slide guitar from Gary Thistlethwaite was a great addition, gave our sound a country tinge and a new lease of life, which led to us doing a show or two around the time – one really good one at Manchester University – Academy 2, a venue we'd played back in the day.

When we haven't played for a long time, we sit in the dressing room beforehand, anxious, full of doubt, asking each other why we are putting ourselves through this. Then we play, the crowd are usually very warm and appreciative, and we come off stage thinking, *Why don't we do this more often?* It's a cycle. Anyway, I know Nigel thinks 'Portrait' off *Long Road* is one of our best songs and as the title track is great too – one of Matthew's best lyrically – we were happy with our efforts and 'Long Road' holds its place in the set when we play today.

The quiet period usually lasts around five years, then Matt will start picking up the guitar and saying to us, *'What do you think of this?'* This leads to a reunion of sorts, usually somewhere cold and we start rehearsing a few tunes around the real purpose of the get-together, to have a pint and catch up.

With *Stockholm,* because of time constraints – we all live in different places, work and have families – we didn't seem to have any time to work on the songs properly as a band, so some ideas were loosely worked on, some drums, guitars and keys were played, vocals recorded and then James sat in front of the computer in his studio, working extremely hard trying to pull it all together. 'Stockholm' and 'F.I.L.A' were the standouts for me, with a few of the other tracks being good, but not quite fulfilling their potential.

I think we all prefer a more band/group activity approach to recording if I'm honest – a band being the sum of its parts – which brings us into 2025 and the new album, *Boogie Woogie,* and the way we've picked it up together as a bunch of mates who like doing this. I suppose that's the thing I'm most proud of, not where we got to or where we went, but the type of people we are and the fact that we found each other. In order to find each other we had to be attracted to one another: it takes a certain type of person and mindset to actually start a band, to arrange to go to the same poly in order to carry on with it, to play shows early on when it's obvious you're not very good and no one cares, a certain type of belief and resilience to not be scared of failure, to absorb it and keep going, to not think twice about packing in poly to do it full time. All five of us were looking for adventure and needed each other to get there. We really couldn't have done it without each other and we still feel the same about each other now, still wanting to do music together and be looking out for each other nearly 40 years later.

It's very hard to explain how special playing live music can be. Other people seem to like it when we do it, which is amazing – but can you imagine how great it is to actually be up there playing it…with your best friends? There are moments we've had together on stage that can never be taken away; a certain chord change, a particular lyric, an entry into a chorus…eyes meeting, a moment where all five of you are so utterly connected, and at the same time completely lost, together…in the music. I feel privileged to have shared these moments with the other four, an experience and connection that just can't be replicated anywhere else in life. I love them all dearly and don't know where I'd be had I not found the four of them.'

James

'1994. Life after A&M, I was living in Kentish Town, not far from Hampstead Heath. Bumming around in London, swimming a lot at the local pool. I signed on and started wearing glasses. The band carried on under the new name Kingsize Screamer, and we played a few gigs. With me on guitar and Simon on bass. I have no memory of them. Other than it was fun playing the guitar, but despite being with some Milltown Brothers we didn't have the same kind of power or conviction of the Milltown Brothers, and I don't think I ever got the feeling that Kingsize Screamer were going to get signed. I can't remember what my head was like in those days but I'm guessing a bit lost. It's a shame as some of the tunes were good, 'A Lot Like Love' being one.

I met my first wife Kathy in those years and we lived together in Kentish Town. She worked in town at UCL as an intensive care nurse, and I got a job proofreading and stuffing envelopes at a City law firm. One day I bumped into Martin 'Fiddly' Bell from the Wonder Stuff in the local Dartmouth Arms. He'd got his own recording set up at his flat in Tufnell Park, it was an early hard disk recording system, it was all tape before. We wrote and recorded some decent demos, he added some great instrumental performances which got us meeting some A & R people, but nothing came of it. More important, I found out I liked recording better than playing live, and I like playing live. This period of time inspired me to get my own recording equipment and start learning to use it in a songwriting process, daring at last to sing. I wrote quite a few songs in this period, but none of them saw the light of day, and probably never will. When I look at the lyrics, they were all telling me something. I had a deep yearning for peace and a return home.

Having got married, we moved to Blackpool in 1998 – me, my wife and baby daughter. Kathy worked in a high-pressure job and I looked after Rosie, which was an eye-opener, having the care of a one-year-old; taught me a few lessons about responsibilities, parenting and being married. I still had my recording stuff and was writing and demoing, I also worked with some musicians I met in town and formed the Show Ponies; again, it looked like I couldn't abandon music making completely despite a complete change in my situation.

Happy with my family life after the birth of Niamh in 1999 but wanting out of a deadly boring civil service job in the DLA at Warbreck Hill in August 2000, I applied to go back to university through clearing and ended up at UCL, the University of Central Lancashire – studying psychology. This was a good move; I liked studying better second time round and a lot of the material made sense now. I found a way to get around the overwhelming amount of information processing by audio recording the lectures and listening back on the drives to and from uni. I did well and was accepted on a PhD programme about lie detection, which was really interesting and could have been a rewarding career.

My marriage to Kathy ended in 2004, and with a lot of help from my parents I moved back to my hometown, Lancaster, but couldn't really motivate myself to do much. I was looking after my two little girls one week on and one week off, which meant a lot of driving to get them to and from school. I learnt a lot about single parenting from this time. It's hard! I think kids need two parents, and I deeply regret that the divorce was really tough on my beloved daughters. At the same time, the freedom afforded by part-time parenting and a house with a double garage meant a studio. I invested in some new equipment and started working with the band's dear friend from school, Max, on a musical project called the Girl El Paranzo, which eventually became a short film directed by Matt from the band. The songs for this were some of my best work; Max is a quite amazing lyricist and there was a nice flow to everything. This was definitely a big development for my recording skills and there followed a handful of film music projects as Fizzy Days and then adverts and music beds with Barney as Dexterous Music, put our way by Matt who was doing Space Digital in Manchester. Being back in Lancaster was really cool and I'd see Nian and his wife Jo every now and again. Recording *Rubberband* in Colne was quite fun and a little bit of a Milltown Brothers revival. Playing bass occasionally for Barney and the Rubbish and supporting Status Quo were memories from around this period too.

When ex-Blue singer Simon Webbe was looking for songs for his *Sanctuary* album, Barney came up with 'Pusherman' and with Max we worked on 'She Is So Unusual' too, recording them in London with Simon and some great engineers. I liked seeing how productions were made ten years on and watching and learning from Simon Webbe's work on singing these songs. Neither song made it on to *Sanctuary* fully, but 'Pusherman' is the hidden track on the release. It was a bit of glamour to go to the launch party in some posh club and take Max. It was like back in the day a bit, but now I could leave it behind.

In 2008 the PhD was abandoned; academia to me looked like it wanted to be a little bit rock 'n' roll but was ridiculously narrow in its view. Barney and I had more or less stopped doing adverts and music, and I got a job at Beaumont College as a music tutor.

This was now the Scope-run FE college for young people with Profound and Multiple Learning Disabilities (PMLD). The place where me and Nian had played our first gig as Warning in 1985. It was an emotionally very demanding but really rewarding job. We founded BCR, a record company, with the students and staff. The students wrote songs about their lives, and we went on mini tours to perform the music. Interestingly these young people, many of whom are non-verbal, are very musical when you can tune into how they communicate. Sometimes we would have very transcendent sessions just making music for an hour or so with these students in wheelchairs using SoundBeam or switches to trigger sounds with input from staff over a slow groove. It was very peaceful and fulfilling for everyone in the room. I met Toni here in 2009 and we married in 2011.

During this time I learned to meditate after reading *The Power of Now* by Eckhart Tolle. Purely by chance I had just met Ian 'Scotty' Moorhouse, a really old friend of Nian's and a local didgeridoo player and we formed Greenheart. We went to Dent Meditation Centre to do some recording and I met the director Eliza, who became my meditation teacher. With Toni, we learned to teach meditation and I became a lot more spiritually aware than I'd ever been before. I'd been through rock 'n' roll, parenting, higher education in psychology and now disability arts. Meditation tied all these elements together for me. Toni and I did a lot of courses on the Beatitudes, the Kabbalah, and teachings in Aramaic. Spirituality became a big thing for us. Greenheart was my musical outlet.

In 2013 the next wave of kids started to arrive, with young Vini born in Lancaster Infirmary. Having a son was really mind-blowing, as was the quite intense spiritual training his mum and I were on at the time. I ended up in southern Spain for a few months at the end of 2014, partly completing some spiritual training we'd been on, partly wanting to write a book about my experiences of working musically with people with disabilities and partly cat-sitting in a small cortijo in Lancaron. Matthew had been sending ideas for songs since the summer of

2013, and together we demoed a few in my studio; this became *Long Road*. I suggested we record some tracks in Spain and found us a studio in Padul, a little town just south of Granada run by Ernesto Cabello, a very nice man. My Spanish wasn't any better than his English, so it was a confusing back and forth with Google Translate to get the session booked. I don't remember the exact dates Nian, Matt and Simon landed in Malaga, but I think January 2014… Great studio, a nice time and some good performances, but lacking Barney, we came back and finished the album by Christmas 2014, handing the project to local producers/mixers Mark Jones and Mark Phythian.

Long Road sounded really good with Barney adding keys – I'd been hacking through it in Spain, which was an eye-opener, pianos are hard – plus the additional playing of Gary Thistlethwaite's pedal steel. The care and attention the Marks invested really helped too. The title track is very good and when we did a few gigs together it felt good.

Once again we found ourselves unable to retire on the proceeds of our music – yet! I needed to earn, so I took student support jobs and market research jobs with Ipsos Mori. And I hosted a radio show, *Mystery Hour*, on our local station Beyond Radio. This was very good, as it featured musicians and bands from the area – getting them into the station and playing live and asking them about their lives in music. I loved doing this. Fortunately for me, serving a ban for a guest swearing on air, I wasn't at the radio station when our home was flooded in November 2017; I was able to grab some gear before my own studio was trashed. Pro tip: don't go into flood water, it's really dangerous. We had to be rehoused because Toni was very pregnant – another daughter, Arabella was born in 2018, and another, Martha, in 2019, both home births – very peaceful. And so for a while, babies, nappies, working…

Then somehow the Milltown Brothers came to record *Stockholm* in my studio. It was very bitty, as no one had the time to really devote themselves to it, but I still think it was good work that paved the way for our subsequent activity. Like *Rubberband*

and *Long Road*, it has some great moments and we tried to use different musical instruments and collaborate with other musicians; Gary Thistlethwaite again on pedal steel, Tommy McAleer on violin and Adrian Fish on sax.

So come Covid, I've five kids with a big range of ages and a steady job providing support to HE students, I now meditate and have musical projects every now and then, releasing music in a limited but dogged way. I expect nothing in return and enjoy it purely because it's good fun and I'm kind of compelled to create music.

In the summer of 2023, the Milltown Brothers again gathered. Simon was 60 in May and we wanted to rehearse and have a get-together. We did, it was good. We did a gig at Hebden Bridge Trades Club in August. It was sold out and a really good night – an astounding thing for me definitely and, I think, the rest of the band. At the gig in November at Lancaster Kanteena it was clear this audience response was a real thing; there are people out there who like the Milltown Brothers a lot.

But at the time of writing unfortunately my second marriage has ended, I'm back in Lancaster and once again I'm a part-time single parent. This is a bit heartbreaking occasionally, as I really miss my kids and they are quite young to be dealing with this. I know that we'll get used to it again, though. The band have recorded another album in Burnley over the summer and are working on the release for September 2025. The process of this recording has been quite different; more live rather than disintegrated and individual as was the norm back in the '90s; recording drums for two weeks and then adding the other instruments afterwards. This was the gold standard we learned in our '90s recording sessions. While this approach is great for isolating instruments so they can sound as good as possible, it does separate the music in time as the successive instruments are added. Maybe there's something about keeping the performance time locked that will sound more live and present. We've often been described as a good live band – so why not record in this way?

I often wonder why we're still doing this well over 30 years on... How did we get so woven into each others' lives and how does this persist to the present day? We're all middle-aged men now with 13 kids between us and still the same line-up as in 1991. Make that 1987. For me there's loyalty, friendship and brotherhood in this band that's still here when other areas of my life have fallen away. I like being a 56-year-old bass player with a critically acclaimed but commercially disappointing '90s indie band. I watch the faces of the people at our gigs and they're buzzing; this is rewarding. It's a nice thing to be able to do this for others while working with your best friends. My job as a bass player and occasional backing vocalist is important, but I don't find it too difficult nowadays as I feel the Milltown Brothers are more mellow and play with more feeling than we used to. This creates a lot more space than when we were smashing it out in the '90s and affords me time to observe the emotional response of the audience – this is frequently magic and I don't know how I missed it first time round. If we could get this new album in the charts, it would feel like closing a circle and finishing the whole business of being thrown out of the charts. A bit of poetic justice.

I still sometimes wonder what would have happened if we'd bought ourselves some recording equipment and rented a space to work in the days of the large record company advance; a lot of bands do this. We could see that A&M spent a lot of money on studios and dimly realised we'd have to pay it back one day. I'd been watching all these producers and engineers in amazingly equipped studios doing their thing and had enjoyed demoing a few ideas on Barney's Korg M1 which had a built-in sequencer (very hi-tech in 1990). So I could see that this was a possible way to go – we could play well, but could we learn to produce our own stuff and develop as a studio band if we had the gear? Spending thousands on a tape machine desk and mics didn't happen, but we did get a 4-track to be fair. Best thing done on that was 'Flowers'. We may have developed our production skills if this had happened, but equally it may have been a terrible idea to let us loose on sensitive expensive equipment. Who knows?

And now I'm sitting in the van heading south on the M6 to London to play at the Lexington. We've done this journey a lot since the late '80s; the only new features are that there's smart motorways south of Manchester now and everyone is on their phones instead of the Walkmans we used back in the day. Otherwise the same relaxed atmosphere is here. This is not a stressful band to be in, for me at least. I wonder what it all means?'

Matthew

'For You

Take me back, take me back
To the time where I began,
Take me back, take me back,
I was lonely then, I know,

You were there when I lost.
A fallen tree with no roots.
You were there when I lost.
You were there to mend my broken soul.

Take me back, take me back
To the place where I belong,
Take me back, take me back.
I was the only boy,

You were there when I lost.
A fallen tree with no roots.
You were there when I lost.
You were there to mend my broken soul.

Writing that was easy. The rest of this – along with all the exams I've ever taken – is the most and the most difficult words I've ever written. I'm no good when I have to remember and explain anything.

But looking back, it was a seven-year recovery. The first bit spent drinking and thinking you can get back to where you were, the next bit formulating a plan of what you are going to do instead, then the last bit trying to get something going, planned or otherwise.

I luckily met Janine in April 1993. A friend of mine invited me out in Burnley at the last minute and we met at the Ritz in Burnley. We've been together since. In 1994 we moved to London, Janine trained to be a journalist and got a job as a junior reporter on the *Islington Gazette*, eventually becoming editor. I still had vague aspirations of resurrecting the band at this point. We were called Kingsize Screamer with James on guitar and Simon on bass. Nian played drums but was living with a partner at the time and needed a job, and it made sense for him to re-enter civilisation, so at some point he left and it was our idea, not his.

Janine would go to work and I'd look in the general appointments of the *Evening Standard* for some work. Winters in London with no money can be tough. Luckily Janine's job involved her reviewing theatres, restaurants and cinema releases, so we spent a lot of time going out to shows and eating nice meals, neither of which we could afford. This was our social life. After a year dundering around doing odd jobs from market research to telesales to bike couriering around central London, Nian got me some work at the company where he was working, Liza Bruce swimwear. I'd do odd jobs for him, including one day driving a van load of models in swimwear to the Grosvenor Hotel on Park Lane to make a protest outside Marks and Spencer's annual shareholder meeting. M&S had apparently copied a design of Liza Bruce's. We arrived and there was already a protest against their suppliers' fishing methods for tinned tuna going on, which was killing dolphins. We joined forces and spent the afternoon chanting *'Marks & Spencer stop the bloody slaughter'* while the paparazzi homed in on the models in swimwear. Light relief in an otherwise dull and bitty working life. Eventually the music faded: Simon and I had a last stand at Canterbury with a father and son rhythm section playing god knows what while I staggered around pissed. No more. It's over. Enough!

I had to do something, and having been exposed to the world of fashion I decided to go and get some sort of qualification to allow me to get back on the straight and narrow. I spent three years at the London College of Fashion studying media in fashion – mixing with precocious 19-year-olds for a subject I had very little interest in. Nineteen-year-olds with Barbie pencil cases and I had a morbid fear of public speaking. How is that possible? How or why I stuck this out, I have no idea. At the same time I got a job working at Next on Oxford Street and Janine's career at the *Islington Gazette* went from strength to strength. It's fair to say Janine kept the ship afloat at this point; I shudder to think where I would have been without her. She is the most honest and straightforward person. I'm very lucky to have met her, love her very much and have so much to thank her for. I'll make sure she reads at least this part of the book.

If I'm honest, I probably still deep down thought a career in music was possible! So at the backend of my degree we formed a band – me, Simon, Nian with Simon's work colleague Steve Taylor on bass. James had moved north to Blackpool. We started as the Milltown Brothers but after a bit became Milo. In 1998 I finished the degree with a 2:2, the whole experience reaffirming education is not for me.

I was 30 and no further on with knowing what I was going do. In July 1998 Janine and I married and two days after getting back from honeymoon out of nowhere I was offered a day's running in a London film company that led to a week's running with another film company called The Mob. Well, I say out out of nowhere; it was the fan of the band who'd written the letter to the *NME* complaining about our '*much ignored demise*' who fixed it up for me, and sorry, I can't even remember her name… If you're reading this, I can't thank you enough: you gave me a future even though running is the bottom rung of a tall ladder in the film industry, you spend all day on your feet doing all the crap jobs anyone needs doing and they're very long days.

Here I met Jonathan Brooke who inspired me to move into the film industry, even though he was about to give it up himself – he'd been put through the rinser working like a dog for two years and grown to hate the culture of commercial film production. A Cambridge graduate, very bright, he gave me a grounding in what was required. I ended up working in the London film business for three years at Channel 4, The Mob, Harry Nash and on the feature film *Kiss Kiss Bang Bang*. Robert Downey Jr. and Val Kilmer who'd played Jim Morrison in the making of *The Doors* movie were in it, but my contribution was completely ignored by IMDb, who don't even feature me in the 54 *'Additional Crew'* members.

During this time Milo played quite a few gigs around London and were managed by Ciro Romano, who gave us back some belief in ourselves. A special mention here to Steve Taylor, a wonderful man. He was great for us, as he gave us a different approach to music – he was also highly intelligent, cool, and held a healthy disregard for petty authority. He sadly died a few years ago. Milo did pretty well, but when Island Records eventually passed on us, the penny dropped and I gave up trying to be in the music business. It was over, end of the line. No more!

After a few years of trying, Janine got pregnant and we decided to relocate back north. In 2001 Harry our first son was born and I got a job at Granada Studios working in the graphics, VFX and production department. I met some great people here and enjoyed working on shows such as *Ant & Dec*, *Coronation Street*, *Stars In Their Eyes* and countless dramas and documentaries. In 2005 Kitt our second child was born, Janine started her own businesses (Women on Wine and Practical PR) and we bought a house. While I was at Granada, I met this charming character called Nigel Wood, who had been forced to work with me as part of a deal his agency's client, the Co-operative Bank, had with Granada. We discovered we got on very well and I've known him ever since.

We had many hilarious and terrifying times together, both at Granada and later on when I started Space Digital. We left a big meeting to sort something serious and sensitive out, went to the Granada café for somewhere quiet, only for the whole thing to be ambushed by a loud, boisterous and energised Jeremy Kyle and his entourage after he'd just finished his talk show, at the time crazily popular. Another time we were doing an ad for the Co-op focusing on their ethical credentials and we'd made this huge globe of old TVs at least four metres high, through which we were going to show a load of edgy documentary clips from all over the place showing various abuses of the planet and human rights around the world. The budget was either spent or assigned, deadline was looming and we'd all – including Nigel and a great character called Kelvin Collins who worked for the bank – assumed we'd do the obvious thing, putting the films on the TVs using CGI in post-production, until the director we were using, another character called Marc Evans, who's made quite a few memorable films and TV programmes, including *My Little Eye* and *Hinterland*, insisted in this big meeting there'd be no film unless we did it all in camera, which meant repairing and wiring up these broken TVs and old monitors in this huge globe and projecting the films through them simultaneously. We were surrounded by glass on the top floor of the CIS Tower, which had once been the tallest building in Manchester, and I remember how pale Nigel – who is terrified of heights – and Kelvin looked, as the three of us scuttled out to discuss the tiny chance of us being able to do this and keep Kelvin in a job.

By this time we'd also managed to make the third Milltown Brothers album, 11 years after *Valve*. I'd always kept writing songs but had no outlet for them. *Rubberband* was produced in Colne by Glen Skinner and it was great to get the band back together and brother Mark got involved too. Personality-wise Mark is the rock star I always wanted to be. Both Simon and I still defer to him as the man of the family. He's the organiser, the enforcer and all-round good guy. We did some gigs which were generally well received, and reacquainted ourselves with some lovely fans we hadn't seen in a while. After the gigs there was a prolonged finishing process for the album: our enthusiasm seemed to wane, real life took over and the Milltown Brothers was again on the back burner. Surely this time it was over! Three albums is a respectable body of work, enough is enough – the end... Time to move on.

James at this point had been writing songs with our old school friend Max and come up with a concept called the Girl El Paranzo. This eventually becoming a short film idea, I pulled in some favours from my film connections and directed it. Barney and his backside is in it too! Wherever Barney goes – so does his arse. Barney should have been the front man of the band – he's the one member who has genuine star quality. Nian might even have been doing the running for this, so you could call it another Milltown Brothers happening.

After five years at Granada, I left to set up Space Digital with two colleagues from there, Matt Wood and Simon Blackledge, both very talented creative people. By this point I was no longer the creative lead, I was the production support. Space Digital got off the ground with the proceeds from a viral film given to us by the writer of this book to demonstrate the lifelike picture of Panasonic Viera TVs, which involved an elephant ejaculating out of the TV screen all over an astonished viewer – since which we've been at it for almost 20 years, travelling all over the world, producing TV adverts and films for companies like the Co-operative Bank and Castrol, VFX for TV shows such as *Dr Who*, *Dracula*, *Ashes to Ashes* and *Fool Me Once*. I've worked with and met some great people – including Nian on and off for film shoots; he does all the organising, has an eye for detail and keeps everything moving forward. Drummers, eh? We've been close friends for many years and it's a privilege to know him – the voice of reason in the band.

In 2011, we had our third child, daughter Marnie. Her birth seemed to stir me to start writing again, I'd play and write songs for hours while she stared out from her cot. All the lyrics seemed to be quite autobiographical, inspired by family life and the passing of time. Eventually I took the plunge and played them to the lads – I was a bit nervous if I'm honest because the lyrics were quite personal. All seemed to go well, and this resulted in us getting together again to record a new album. Jim was spending the winter in Spain – he found a recording studio and we went out to meet him. We finished the album in Oswaldtwistle at Mark Jones' studio – he did a great job pulling it all together – and I think *Long Road* is up there with *Slinky* as our best album… so far, thanks to Andy Hayward for the front cover, a painting by him of his son, Josh – not, as some assume, me. Andy's dad John is a big fan of the band.

After *Long Road*, although nobody said anything, we quietly decided we'd keep the band ticking along. It's a privilege to be able to meet up with your friends and do something together that has a history and you enjoy doing. Nothing has changed that much in our behaviour or relationship to each other: a cool, safe place to mess around and let off steam!

In 2019 we decided to do another album. Fraz (Jim, James, Hairy Dogman, take your pick) fancied producing it at his own home studio. Over the summer of 2019 we'd head up to Lancaster to record. Because of the studio size we had to do a lot of the parts individually, so it took time and the burden fell heavily on Jim's shoulders. Then Covid came, so he literally was on his own mixing and finishing the album. I've always felt a little guilty that Jim had to play the bass in the band, he is a great guitarist in his own right. At school we'd write songs together and musically and as a friend I've always felt very close to him. He's very spiritual, has a great sense of humour – a great guy. He did a real job and there's a lot of good stuff on *Stockholm*, the album that was the result.

We released it ourselves, didn't really promote it and things went quiet with the band – I still kept writing as did the other band members. Eventually Simon decided it was time to play some gigs, which we really hadn't done many of in the last 25 years. Simon is the background driving force behind the band, the sensible one, although he can be mildly eccentric at times too. He's really made my life in the band easy, we've written some great songs together and ever since he made me feel great when he talked to me about the Spire's 'Salford Lady', he's pushed me to do things I probably wouldn't have done without him, including actually crapping in my pants when I first went on stage in the south of France with him in 1985. The wisest and most pleasant of us all, a great brother in every sense.

Jonathan got involved as usual and we booked a gig at the Kanteena in Lancaster and Trades Club in Hebden Bridge and completely surprised ourselves by selling both out! It was great to play again in front of familiar and new faces. We booked more gigs and again people kept coming – very humbling. On the back of this we decided to make another album, our sixth, and Nigel came along and said he had an idea and wanted to write a book – and he didn't want to be paid – so we thought: *Why not*, and to his surprise he got a publishing deal. He's a very creative, dogged and inspiring fellow and I'm lucky to know him.

And now the album is recorded, we're waiting on the mixes and a September 2025 release date looms. We appear, thanks to Jonathan, to have a different kind of record company – *Last Night From Glasgow* – to promote and distribute it and we have dates to play more gigs and hang out.

Looking to the future, I hope and am sure I'll do more of this Milltown Brothers thing, a bit more work, and most important of all spend time with my wife and kids… Harry went to Sheffield University and got a first class degree. Kitt started playing football for Preston North End when he was 8 and 11 years later is close to breaking into their first team, and Marnie loves athletics and hockey and has a very happy nature.

I got lucky.'

Simon

'As I lie in bed on a colder than in the past few weeks November morning some 30 or so years since the so-called *'much ignored demise'* of the Milltown Brothers, on the cusp of retirement in my early 60s, enjoying the highs and lows of having my two grown-up sons living back at home with me and my wife Rachel (who is also about to retire), I find myself experiencing the same relationship with the Milltown Brothers that there ever was: incredibly partisan support, obsession, brotherhood, pride and a vague undertow of melancholy and anxiety.

There's no safety net for bands when they lose their record deal, when the numbers at the gigs trickle away and are separated by large stretches of nothing and there's nothing to talk about either. Watching some programme about boy bands the other day – not that the Milltown Brothers were a boy band, even though we were indeed boys; well, at least the others were when we started – I saw Simon Cowell saying, *"If you're involved in the music business you have to expect the lows if you've enjoyed the highs, and if you can't you should be an accountant (like my dad"* ... or words to that effect. He's right – roll with the punches, pick yourself up and dust yourself off and all those old platitudes... true of course, but actually not very helpful. Drinking copious cans of Holsten Pils at home every night, avoiding looking at the music press and getting up at midday – that does the trick, at least for a few months. The more you do that, the further away you get from real life and the deeper you get into a relationship with self-pity and resentment.

All the while our contemporaries were soaring and riding the new Britpop wave – Ocean Colour Scene had a huge album, Oasis and Blur fought it out in the tabloid press to be the global kings of the scene, Shed Seven picked up the pieces and are smashing it now. Good for them. Me and Matthew played with a father and son rhythm section in a students' union in Canterbury some evening in late 1995 to bemused onlookers, wondering how four individuals could be playing different songs at the same time. I was sober and endured the tormented public death rattle of the band; we were atrocious.

Everyone will sort of know how it feels in their own way – having something or someone you really loved, who brought you out of yourself, helped you overcome your shyness, your hang-ups, helped to mitigate or hide your vulnerabilities, empowered you, helped you see the world and what seemed like the world wanted to see you, made you feel valued, loved, challenged, stretched, fulfilled and alive… like you had a purpose, then it all goes horribly wrong and they're gone and now, at least for a bit, you might as well be… No really dark and serious suicidal thoughts for me, but it does cross one's mind… paranoid, jealous, angry, anxious, denied… lost.

So, what happened to me after 1994? When Nigel asked me to contribute this bit myself, I was put in mind of the scene in Monty Python's *The Meaning of Life* when, after the Mr Creosote sketch, the camera follows Eric Idle acting the part of a French waiter who starts to tell the story of his life, urging us to follow him back to where it all began; to the moments of his time that formed him – as he walks down a field towards a cottage, the camera slows and turns away and the film moves to the next scene with him desperately and vainly trying to regain our attention.

When the nice advance from our final publishing deal with Rondor ran out, it was get a job time, and after half-heartedly trying to retain a foothold in the music industry with failed applications to the likes of Gibson Guitars and Phil McIntyre Entertainments I stumbled into market research by mistake and stayed there for 30 years. I responded to a classified ad in the *Evening Standard* – 'French Interviewers Wanted' – thinking I'd be able to put my degree to good use in some glamorous journalistic milieu. What I actually ended up doing was persuading deeply reluctant British white van owners to be interviewed by me over the phone, from a call centre in a down-at-heel market research field agency in Islington. My supervisor had been a fan of the band and couldn't believe I was working for him.

Rachel and me had been married for a couple of years and living in a one-bedroom flat in Cornwallis Square, off the upper end of the Holloway Road. She was just getting going in the Mod Brit department at Christie's auctioneers, and I was under increasing pressure to contribute to household finances and get some self-respect back – and no excuse not to do so with the band, even from an extremely optimistic viewpoint, firmly on a low light back burner.

I eventually settled into working life. Firstly, as a telephone interviewer moving to full-time as a field 'executive' (there are great make-you-feel-good job titles in the market research industry) then as a junior researcher and, by around 2004, as a research director. For the first six or so years working at Gordon Simmons Research and then Opinion Research Corporation International – grand company names too – I still garnered strong ambitions of getting back into the music business. Indeed, during the period 1994 to 2001 along with Matthew, Nian, James and a small group of musicians including the fondly remembered two Stephens – one Lloyd Cole's drummer, the other the unfortunately no longer with us bass player Steve Taylor, who I'd met at work – we had a few nearly moments, the majority with Milo.

All of this undermined my efforts as a researcher, thoroughly distracting me and probably making me the bore of the office as I would all too often, especially after work drinking sessions at the Red Lion on St John Street, Islington, regale colleagues about my days in the band and how Oasis supported us and how we played on the same bill as Nirvana and were on *Wogan*... that fading glory was what I was clinging to. I remember getting off the train at Cannon Street (Rachel and me had moved to Kent in 1996 first to Tonbridge, then Tunbridge Wells) and descending the escalator at 8 a.m, staring at the silver of the metalled ceiling and thinking the fractured me among the shimmer of reflected light was somehow my artistic essence evaporating in this métro-boulot-dodo dystopia... yes, I agree, you get very self-obsessed and deluded when you're dropped from (even a modest) height by the music business. Getting over yourself is something we all have to do, but Pentonville Road helped.

In 2000 we moved back to London and settled again in Pimlico. Somehow I grew up: 9/11 happened, we had our first son Alexander in January 2002 and I started to take the job more seriously and was rewarded financially and involved in more interesting projects that took me to some great places and new experiences – three days holed up in an Abidjan hotel in the Ivory Coast with a full-on coup d'état occurring outside, for example.

However, at the beginning of this phase, Matthew had written a song called 'Cloud Nine' after the birth of his first son Harry, and even though he was back up north, we started to write songs again and get together – me doing most of the travelling of course – playing them with whoever was around. James was doing well with the Show Ponies and Barney was going great guns supporting the likes of Status Quo at Wembley Arena with his band the Rubbish... but we eventually managed to get them all involved one way or another – you'd have thought we'd know better, but we'd kept close and in early 2002 we got some finance sorted, unfortunately some of it mine – and recorded *Rubberband* – including, of course, 'Cloud Nine'.

At first it was fun, laying down rhythm tracks during two splendid weeks off work in the Derby Arms in Colne with Glenn Skinner at the production helm and then sporadically, frustratingly, painstakingly slowly overdubbing in Glenn's flat in Streatham for what seemed like an eternity. The album was finally released in the summer of 2004 much after the initial flush of enthusiasm had departed, at which time we mustered only three shows to promote it. In London, the Borderline – very good; Jesus and all that. Manchester, the Roadhouse – quite good. And Accrington, can't remember where – terrible. We never had much luck in Accrington. By the end of the summer the band were ready to go back into hibernation with me personally £5000 down – it can be an expensive hobby.

In March 2004 our second son Jimmy was born; we moved to Elton, near Peterborough in the April; and from the end of that summer through to December 2006, I got my head down with clients and my broader research experience to a point where I was confident enough to branch out as an independent researcher – something I've now been doing for 17 years. I consider it one of my better achievements to have been able to work for myself for so long during which time I fine-tuned my qualitative moderating skills *('if you don't know, you really don't need to know')* and conducted much of my work in French. Nothing beats rock 'n' roll... but it did pay the bills and there were far worse careers

I could have got tangled up in.

Having arrived in Elton, I became a frequenter of Rachel's dad's pub, The Crown – which, back in those days, was very much the place to be. By 2005 I had met Gary Rice, Chris Page and his son Dan and Paul Grist. They'd already been rehearsing as a covers band and asked if I'd join them on bass. What started as a casual thing ended up being 18 years of on/off occasional gigs as The Eltones (named after the village – do you get it?). Fundamentally as a Beatles covers band; we even had the drop T logo on the kick drum skin and would do some of the gigs in costume. We went down a storm in local village halls, marquees and pubs for charity fundraisers, birthday parties and weddings, and much fun was had. There is something to be said for playing really great songs when there's not so much riding on it; when it's just for the crack – when people know every word of the songs you're playing. All you need is love, indeed.

And where was all of the original rock 'n' roll during this period? In fact, working for myself obviously allowed greater freedom to pursue musical projects – one of which, between 2008 and 2011, proved to be enjoyable and pretty fulfilling. With Ash Woodward (guitar) – who supported the Milltown Brothers as recently as 2023 – Neil Gordon (bass) and Ryan Vann (drums) I performed with Sixtyfivemiles. So called because of the distance between Elton and the rehearsal room in Ash and Neil's hometown of Atherstone in Warwickshire. Me doing the travelling again. We had a blast and recorded an album, *Finnish Tango,* and *The Mary* EP, both released through Cherry Red and still available on all the digital platforms if anyone is interested. I've a thing about Mary.

It was strange to be on lead vocals again with main songwriting duties, back to Tropical Blue and the Word Association days. Most of our gigs were in the West Midlands but, despite giving it a good crack, we didn't really break out of the regional indie circuit. In early 2011 we were booked to support David McAlmont at Birmingham Academy 3. Dutifully we showed up, watched his soundcheck and then he watched ours. Having returned to the dressing room with the gear ready to go and doors at 7.30 p.m., we had a visit from the promoter who informed us David didn't want a support band that night and that we were free to go… Maybe he was intimidated or maybe we were too loud – whatever, the writing was on the wall. Indeed, it was probably foolish of me, aged 47, to think I could become an indie kid crowd-pleaser, so by summer of that year the band Sixtyfivemiles was no more.

But the fact is through time, the Milltown Brothers stayed among us. For me it remained a dominant force. Even if we were doing other stuff, not rehearsing, songwriting, gigging or record-ing, doing nothing at all, we'd always find an excuse to meet up, have some beers and chew the fat… much of which would inevitably be reflections on how things were, what we missed, but we've got better at the positives of it. The bottom line is we enjoy each other's company, make each other laugh and have so much in common, especially the past – drawn together in a 'musical brotherhood' – and it keeps poking its nose into the present and future too, all of which might go some way to explaining why the five of us together always feels musically amazingly good. It's a privilege to be involved. We've been blown away by the support and love shown by everyone who has attended the recent gigs, and we are lucky people are still willing to come along and enjoy the tunes after all these years.

One way and another the Milltown Brothers returned with two more albums between 2011 and 2020, both with songs writ-ten exclusively by Matthew: *Long Road* (2015) and *Stockholm* (2020). It's a source of regret and frustration for me that the two of us have not been very productive as a songwriting unit in recent years although on our forthcoming album – *Boogie Woogie* – there are a couple of collaborations. Back in the day, when we were together for longer and more often, there was so much opportunity to do it. But like most things, you only realise how much you didn't take advantage of it when it's gone.

Notwithstanding that part of it, fun is still there to be had; not least in the shape of a week away in a Spanish residential studio in Padul, just south of Granada, recording some backing tracks for *Long Road* in January 2014. We're all pretty proud of both *Long Road* and *Stockholm*; both were self-financed, self-organised and self-promoted (with plenty of help from Jonathan and a bit from a press plugger on *Long Road*). The former was produced by Mark Jones and Mark Phythian, with *Stockholm's* production in the hands of James working out of his home studio – otherwise known as his soundproofed garage, in Galgate, Lancaster.

All the while, we were getting our children through school while holding down what have been, at times, stressful jobs and witnessing a golden period for Burnley Football Club as we returned to the top flight for the first time in over 30 years and have pretty much stayed there ever since. UTC! (That's Up The Clarets!) My eldest, Alexander, who accompanies me to games when it works for us both has known nothing but relative success for the club – I have to remind him that I was there on the Bee Hole End on 9 May 1987 when goals from Ian Grewcock and Ian Britton secured a 2-1 victory over Leyton Orient, giving us sufficient points to remain in the Football League.

So back to this chilly early November morning in 2024 and the Milltown Brothers are roughly centre stage in my life again (they are never off it if truth be told). Strange how things are turning out. I'm pretty much retired, we've been gigging again with more coming up and an album waiting to be finished with a release date planned for… sometime in 2025… and a book being written about us – who'd have thought!? When Nigel originally suggested the idea to Matthew in December 2023, we were all intrigued by it – even if we were concerned what people might think about a band as anonymous as we became thinking they merited having a book written about them. Unfortunately, my life had been clouded by some news that probably made me a little keener for him to do it.

The news was I'd been diagnosed as having scleroderma, which can be quite a serious genetic condition that causes skin and tissue to harden. I have the diffuse systemic type which means not only my extremities but my internal organs can be affected by it, but so far so good. I've had to adapt my guitar playing a little, but it's excellent exercise and am doing great… the really good news, of course, is if you come to a gig and I mess up, I've now got the perfect excuse!

Of course, I can't end this without thanking my wife Rachel and two sons for putting up with me – or should I say without me – over the years. My physical and emotional absences, on the road, always gigging, recording and rehearsing, usually somewhere that required me to be away overnight or for days on end, and even with my 'proper job' I was often travelling extensively when the children were very young. Rachel has the patience of a saint and I'm so lucky to have met her and had all that support and forbearance. She is the only one of the band members' partners to have lived the Milltown Brothers story in its entirety. That alone marks her out as unique.'

Mark

'My sense of the past is more holistic, or blob-like, than timeline, so this is murky. People, places and happenings massively important in the moment become blurred in a homogeneous maelstrom of memories. Those that are fact, those that are based on the truth but have been adorned and elaborated by my mind over time, and all usually deeply emotional.

My life in rugby union has included representing England Schools, winning the Premiership and European Shield as Backs Coach for Sale Sharks and being Director of Rugby at Orrell, and since my somewhat paradoxical artistic life has involved not only painting, music making and, don't mention it down at the club, poetry, the pea soup my mind makes of it today is… well I'm occasionally asked about it for articles and reference information and I'm pretty useless. All exacerbated by the fact that my personal life has, shall we say, been a roller coaster too.

So if I can't clarify my own trip along the road, I've got no chance with the Milltown Brothers, but it's had a huge impact and continues to have on the Nelson family, even if my involvement through teaching Simon and Matthew how to play, playing that gig as the Millionaire Brothers with Simon, watching them play so many times and making music with them and the rest of the band over the years, has just become a big lump of stuff from which things leap almost at random. It has just been there in my life, obviously through Matt and Simon being my brothers and we've always been close, but also with Barney in various guises. I've also played in a one-off combo with Nian and Fraz at the school I taught at and was a colleague of Nian's mother at the same school in Lancaster. You can see how everything is intertwined. Back in Colne I got involved and close to the recording of *Rubberband*, in the upstairs room at the Derby Arms pub in the town; I even have a part-writing credit on 'Sunday Morning'. My girlfriend at the time helped fund the album as well as a longish-term band I was in with Barney in the later years, when it was in its final iteration, Red Squared. Me and Matthew played quite a few sets in the Derby Arms and other places in the town as part of the annual Colne Blues Festival. The Milltown Brothers headlined the charity concert we oddly named And Finally… at the Muni, Colne in 2009 …where Big Picture, another band I was part of along with Barney again, also played.

I know I was always envious about their links with Burnley FC and football in general. I'm indelibly linked to rugby union and no matter how you try in terms of art and music it simply doesn't work. The Milltowns have never played a full-blown gig at Turf Moor, but not so many years ago they played in the Fan Zone before a game against Leicester in the Premier League. It was great they just about played Turf Moor – as opposed to Def Leppard, born and bred in Sheffield, Yorkshire, who were portrayed as playing there in the film *Bank of Dave*… but never actually did.

Deep into the writing of this book, Nigel came to talk about some stuff – and as we chatted, out of the murk of my mind came a review in *NME* about the Milltowns playing the Marquee. I remembered because of the opening sentence 'And Jesus Danced…' and explained to him I couldn't work it out, I didn't know what was going on. I even asked a colleague, the Head of English, what he thought. He said it was probably a young journalist trying to show off starting a sentence with 'And'. I thought maybe a reference to Matthew's occasional Messiah-like stance on stage. It turned out it was about a hippy dude who turned up at music events and gigs all over London and if he danced it was good. Next thing Nigel's telling me it would be a brilliant name for this book. It had been called *A Little Bit Wonderful* for ages – a title Nigel was so wedded to he'd bought the URL, but I'm chuffed I helped him waste his money.

But truth is. the last two band gigs I went to in 2024 in Rawtenstall and Barnoldswick are in the same place in my head as that review. I have no concept of old and new with the band. It is just there. Matthew and Simon say they have a mantra within the band: *'check out any time you like but you can never leave.'* I like the concept. In that whatever band members do, they are always linked back to a core. It's like that in sport. The special teams are made up of gifted individuals. These players can leave and join other clubs or quit playing but they will always have a bond back to the mothership of the special team. And they most likely played at their peak in that special team, feeding off the other players… Age and time can take many things, but it can never take that shared experience away. The feeling, not the detail. The Milltown Brothers, from my perspective, have always been and will always be a creative force. They could still have a hit album, they could still headline Glastonbury, they could still play at Turf Moor. And there's a bond between the five of them that rivals any team spirit I've come across in their more laid-back, only occasionally frenzied way, and particularly with Matthew and Simon there is a band-focused creative energy and flame that won't go out. It's all driven by a bit of regret, I guess, but that's understandable. They touched the fire.

That said, with Matthew's songwriting I'm not sure his over-riding intention is a yearning for them to reach an audience. His songs are articulate and insightful, both lyrically and melodically, personal and observational. Simon has always evolved them musically as well as writing songs in his own right. The same can be said of Barney and Fraz who also write their own songs; in truth, I'm not sure if Nian is a songwriter, but he's a bloody great drummer.

The result remains a great mixture of musical excellence and melodic harmonies wrapped up with a big bunch of emotional mates' stuff which naturally amplifies many folds in the family. That hasn't changed since their first forays as a band. So much time may have passed, the style may have evolved, but the brotherly soul remains at the heart of everything, like all great teams.'

Part 7
AFTER (2025–)

Boogie Woogie

The Milltown Brothers' sixth album of new songs was released September 2025. The first time any were played to a live audience was at gigs in May 2025 at the 100 Club on Oxford Street and Trades Club, Hebden Bridge. Each song was recorded live at Chris Lewis's Groove Studio in Burnley, in a few weeks scattered throughout the summer of 2024, with all the band playing together, in a handful of takes. Previously, they'd followed the industry norm, painstakingly laying down drums, then each instrument separately and finally vocals, over days and weeks, to get the 'best' version of each. The aim with *Boogie Woogie* was to get the best version of the band playing together, not the best version of each element that comprised the band mixed together. The opening track and first single, 'Bring It On', was released in May 2025. The more rootsy, stoical yet familiar groove, emphatically middle-aged men keeping the flame not just flickering but vibrantly burning, is highlighted by the liberal use of banjo alongside a more relaxed, confident delivery – less yearning more accepting.

'Bring It On'
'Time To Move On'
'Grab The Sun'
'Mother's Cooking'
'Hi Lo'
'She Loves You'
'Fool (Too Much In Love With The World)'
'Golden Key'

'Again And Again'
'Your World Is Changing'
'Harbour Town'

After the straightforward 'Long Road' and 'Stockholm', the opening tracks on their most recent new albums (2015 and 2020 respectively), *Boogie Woogie* returns the band to the territory of the slightly disconcerting album title, exemplified by first album *Slinky* in 1991. As there was then, there is a strange method to the madness. *Boogie Woogie* is Barney's favourite genre of music, so much so that's he has it tattooed in unflattering large letters across the top of his bottom. The original idea, if that's what you'd call it, was to have this image as the album cover.

But Matthew – the owner of the idea – was persuaded it was taking things too far, it had nothing to do with the Milltown Brothers music, other than by way of Barney's fingertips, so they opted for a plain yet optimistic, late '60s psychedelic typography. It seems the phrase has evolved to become descriptive of a spontaneous feeling among the band, expressing joyous, disbelief they are alive and kicking and still making music together.

WHAT IF?

30 August 1991, Nijmigen

There is no what if. Things would've been different. And different again. And again and again. We all could be anywhere or indeed nowhere.

Milltown Brothers was unfortunate.

But the Milltown Brothers were ridiculously lucky.

Then they were unlucky.

They did what they did, they made (and continue to make) their choices, good and not so good, and this is what happened to them.

But this band of brothers is a heartwarming, persistent and human thing. Not particularly commensurate with global success, power, wealth and influence. Which is what, by 1991, the Milltown Brothers were just about expecting and expected to achieve. But what has it brought the musicians, bands and indeed celebrities and superstars in sport, film, the arts and all walks of life? All manner of fates alongside the positives. Death. Incarceration. Suicide. Insanity. Troubles. Exploitation. Division. Hate. Addiction. Envy. Assassination. Ruin. Hell. Isolation. Paranoia. Ridicule.

None of which would have put the Milltown Brothers off the idea at the time.

The Milltown Brothers have been one of the luckiest bands in the world. They're alive. They've a couple of handfuls of songs to bear comparison with many of the most successful musicians and bands of any era and may yet make more. They've all had at least as happy and fulfilling lives as – on balance – anyone has a right to expect. The Milltown Brothers is still a huge amount of fun and they are still very much brothers. They've had more than their fair share of the thing that happens when you're doing something else. Happiness. And they can still make magic together. It's cast a little light over every part of their lives. And a few other people's too.

What more could you hope for? Other than Jesus dancing twice.

* * *

3 May 2024, Rawtenstall

A bunch of people find each other.
They become a band of brothers.
The band find they can soar.
The band that can soar gets lucky.
Things are a little bit wonderful.
The band that can soar gets unlucky
And must find something else to do.
But still make bits of magic in-between
And realise a little bit wonderful
Is all it ever needed to be.

EPILOGUE

It wasn't cloudy, cold and rainy on the day Icarus managed to escape the Minotaur, so he didn't fly straight home as fast as he could flap to escape the cold, the wet and the Minotaur. And he didn't live happily ever after or have children.

Many of the Milltown Brothers' children have been to at least one of their gigs. Witnessed the magic and joy. It's incredible their dads did this all the time all over the place when they were no older than some of them. But they did and their children know.

APPENDIX

Gigs

1988
January	Rosebank Hall, Didsbury
February	Caernarvon Castle, Camden
March	Sir George Robey, Finsbury Park
March	New Pegasus, Stoke Newington
29 March	Rock Garden, Covent Garden
29 April	Hype Club, Bull & Gate, Kentish Town
6 May	New Pegasus, Stoke Newington
14 May	Boardwalk, Manchester
1 June	Dingwalls, Camden
10 June	Selwyn College, Cambridge
June	Hype Club, Bull & Gate, Kentish Town
June	Manchester Polytechnic
26 June	Rock Garden, Covent Garden
27 August	The Greyhound, Fulham
15 September	Boardwalk, Manchester
17 September	Marquee Club, Soho
4 November	Boardwalk, Manchester
1 December	Camden Palace

1989
27 February	Duchess of York, Leeds
28 February	The Jug, Doncaster
2 March	Bangor University
3 March	Mean Fiddler, Harlesden
7 April	The Square, Harlow
21 April	Aberystwyth University
25 April	Chester College
29 April	Warwick University
8 May	Tropic Club, Bristol

9 May	Venue Cardiff
11 May	Moles, Bath
12 May	The Greyhound, Fulham
13 May	Warwick University
14 May	University of Surrey, Guildford
16 May	Leeds Polytechnic
17 May	Boardwalk, Manchester
18 May	The Sugarhouse, Lancaster
19 May	JB's, Dudley
20 May	The New Adelphi Club, Hull
26 May	Town & Country Club, Kentish Town
6 September	Manchester University
30 September	University of Birmingham
2 October	Dingwalls, Camden
4 October	University of London Union
10 October	Old Times Ipswich
11 October	CCAT Cambridge
12 October	Nene College Northampton
13 October	The Charlotte, Leicester
14 October	Warwick University
17 October	Brighton Polytechnic
18 October	Southampton University
19 October	Oxford Polytechnic
20 October	Moles, Bath
21 October	Boardwalk Manchester
23 October	Bristol Polytechnic
25 October	Wolverhampton Polytechnic
26 October	South Hill Park Arts Centre Bracknell
27 October	JB's, Dudley
28 October	The New Adelphi Club, Hull
29 October	University of Surrey Guildford
30 October	Trent Polytechnic Nottingham
31 October	Kazbah Sunderland
1 November	Huddersfield Polytechnic
2 November	Sheffield University
3 November	The Sugarhouse, Lancaster
4 November	Citadel, St Helens
5 November	Liverpool Polytechnic
7 November	Leeds Polytechnic

8 November	Rock Garden, Covent Garden
9 November	Middlesex Polytechnic, Enfield
10 November	Kent University, Canterbury
19 November	Mean Fiddler, Harlesden
21 November	Gwent College, Newport
22 November	St David's University, Lampeter
23 November	Aberystwyth University
24 November	Polytechnic of Wales, Treforest
25 November	Cardiff University
26 November	Swansea University

1990

20 January	Nottingham University
24 January	Morecambe Gardens
25 January	Sheffield Polytechnic
26 January	Boardwalk, Manchester
27 January	Humberside College Hull
30 January	Birmingham University
2 February	Dorset Institute Bournemouth
3 February	Moles, Bath
4 February	Fleece and Firkin, Bristol
17 March	North Pier Blackpool
6 April	University of London Union
3 May	Salisbury Arts Centre
4 May	Moles, Bath
5 May	Camden Falcon
6 May	University of Surrey, Guildford
8 May	The New Adelphi Club, Hull
9 May	Take Two Sheffield
10 May	Loughborough University
11 May	Birmingham Polytechnic
12 May	Nottingham University
13 May	Fleece and Firkin, Bristol
14 May	Bridge End Arts Centre, Stoke
16 May	The Jug, Doncaster
17 May	Trades Club, Hebden Bridge
20 May	Womad Festival, Morecambe
21 May	Duchess of York, Leeds
23 May	The Old Trout, Windsor

25 May	Wolverhampton Polytechnic
26 May	The Charlotte, Leicester
8 June	The Muni, Colne
16 June	King's College, Cambridge
June	unknown Oxford College Ball
June	PowerHaus, Camden Market
30 June	Manchester International 2
25 August	Reading Festival
6 October	Sunderland Polytechnic
7 October	Lancashire Polytechnic, Preston
8 October	Nottingham Polytechnic
10 October	Sheffield University
11 October	The Sugarhouse, Lancaster
12 October	The Muni, Colne
13 October	Cardiff University
16 October	UMIST, Manchester
18 October	Loughborough University
19 October	University of London Union
23 October	Kent University, Canterbury
24 October	The Richmond, Brighton
25 October	The Joiners Arms, Southampton
26 October	The Square, Harlow
27 October	Warwick University
28 October	Surrey University, Guildford
30 October	Middlesex Polytechnic
31 October	Keele University, Stoke
1 November	Nene College, Northampton
2 November	London School of Economics
3 November	Moles, Bath
4 November	Fleece and Firkin, British
3 December	Town & Country Club, Kentish Town
12 December	Town & Country Club, Kentish Town
28 December	PowerHaus, Camden Market

1991

31 January	Loughborough University
1 February	Lion Street Club, Telford
2 February	The Muni, Colne
5 February	Borderline Soho

7 February	Polytechnic of Wales, Treforest
8 February	Bournemouth Polytechnic
9 February	Moles, Bath
11 February	Boardwalk, Manchester
12 February	Newcastle Polytechnic
13 February	Freetown Club, Stoke
14 February	Sheffield Polytechnic
15 February	Wolverhampton Polytechnic
16 February	Nottingham University
22 February	La Locomotive, Paris
23 February	La Locomotive, Paris
3 March	Parr Hall, Warrington supporting The La's
4 March	Leicester University supporting The La's
5 March	University of East Anglia, Norwich supporting The La's
7 March	Octagon Centre, Sheffield University supporting The La's
8 March	The Hummingbird, Birmingham supporting The La's
9 March	Manchester Academy 1 supporting The La's
11 March	Middlesbrough Town Hall supporting The La's
12 March	The Plaza Glasgow supporting The La's
13 March	The Network, Edinburgh supporting The La's
14 March	Leeds University supporting The La's
16 March	Town & Country Club, Kentish Town supporting The La's
17 March	Town & Country Club, Kentish Town supporting The La's
18 March	The Event, Brighton supporting The La's
20 March	Cambridge Corn Exchange supporting The La's
21 March	Cardiff University supporting The La's
22 March	Royal Court Liverpool supporting The La's
1 May	The Warehouse, Leeds
2 May	The Sugarhouse, Lancaster
3 May	Manchester Academy 2
4 May	The Leadmill, Sheffield
5 May	Nottingham Polytechnic
7 May	Liverpool Polytechnic
8 May	Leicester University

9 May	Cambridge Junction
10 May	University of London Union
11 May	Portsmouth Polytechnic
13 May	Bierkeller, Bristol
14 May	Birmingham University
15 May	Calton Studios, Edinburgh
16 May	Caesar's Palace, Aberdeen
17 May	King Tut's Wah Wah Hut, Glasgow
18 May	King Tut's Wah Wah Hut, Glasgow
19 May	Riverside Newcastle
24 May	The Underworld, Camden
31 May	L'Aéronef, Lille
1 June	Le Plan, Ris-Orangis
3 June	Le Jimmy Bar, Bordeaux
4 June	Le Bikini, Toulouse
5 June	Trans Club, Lyon
7 June	Doornroosje, Nijmijen
8 June	Crystal Palace Bowl supporting The Pixies
9 June	Melkweg Amsterdam
10 June	Schlachthof viertel, Munich
11 June	Luxor, Cologne
12 June	De Effenaar, Eindhoven
15 June	Grosse Freiheit, Hamburg
16 June	Loft Club, Berlin
17 June	B52 Munich
19 June	Le Terminal, Nancy
21 June	La Locomotive, Paris
22 June	Dolce Vita, Lausanne
24 June	Universal Music Festival, Madrid
25 June	Club Sala KGB, Barcelona
10 July	The Astoria, Soho
July	Boston
July	Danceteria, New York
July	Providence
July	San Francisco
23 July	Whisky a Go Go Hollywood
24 July	Bogart's, Long Beach
30 July	CBGBs, New York
24 August	Reading Festival

30 August	Goffertstadion, Nijmigen
31 August	De Doelen, Rotterdam
17 September	Max's Taphouse, Baltimore supporting The Wonder Stuff
18 September	Theatre of the Living Arts, Philadelphia supporting The Wonder Stuff
19 September	Marquee New York supporting The Wonder Stuff
20 September	Fastlane, Asbury Park supporting The Wonder Stuff
21 September	Club Babyhead, Providence supporting The Wonder Stuff
22 September	WNFX's 8th birthday party Boston with Nirvana, Smashing Pumpkins
25 September	DRE Festival, Long Island supporting The Wonder Stuff
26 September	Toad's Place, New Haven supporting The Wonder Stuff
29 September	Club Soda, Montreal supporting The Wonder Stuff
30 September	Penguin Rock Bar, Ottawa supporting The Wonder Stuff
1 October	Hamilton, supporting The Wonder Stuff
2 October	The Opera House, Toronto supporting The Wonder Stuff
3 October	The Opera House, Toronto supporting The Wonder Stuff
4 October	The Opera House, Toronto supporting The Wonder Stuff
5 October	Federation Hall, Waterloo supporting The Wonder Stuff
7 October	Empire Club, Cleveland supporting The Wonder Stuff
9 October	St. Andrews Hall, Detroit supporting The Wonder Stuff
10 October	Cabaret Metro, Chicago supporting The Wonder Stuff

11 October	First Avenue, Minneapolis supporting The Wonder Stuff
14 October	Roseland Theater, Portland supporting The Wonder Stuff
15 October	Commodore Ballroom, Vancouver supporting The Wonder Stuff
16 October	RKCNDY (Rock Candy), Seattle supporting The Wonder Stuff
18 October	I-Beam, San Francisco supporting The Wonder Stuff
19 October	I-Beam, San Francisco supporting The Wonder Stuff
20 October	The Roxy Theatre, Hollywood supporting The Wonder Stuff
21 October	The Roxy Theatre, Hollywood supporting The Wonder Stuff
22 October	The Backdoor Studio, San Diego supporting The Wonder Stuff
November:	Reading University
November	Exeter University
20 December	Burnley Mechanics

1992

19 February	Shinsaibashi Club Quattro, Osaka
20 February	Nagoya Club Quattro
21 February	Shibuya Club Quattro, Tokyo
22 February	Shibuya Club Quattro, Tokyo
23 February	Shibuya Club Quattro, Tokyo
19 March	Leicester University supported by The Wonder Stuff
4 April	Royal Court Liverpool supporting The Charlatans
7 April	Newcastle City Hall supporting The Charlatans
8 April	Manchester Apollo supporting The Charlatans
9 April	The Hummingbird, Birmingham supporting The Charlatans
10 April	Newport Centre supporting The Charlatans
11 April	Brixton Academy supporting The Charlatans

13 April	Cambridge Corn Exchange supporting The Charlatans
April	The Barrowlands, Glasgow supporting The Charlatans
April	Cardiff University supporting The Charlatans
23 May	Lancaster University supporting The Charlatans
18 July	Haldern Pop, Rees-Haldern
16 August	Oak Hill Park, Accrington
21 August	The Muni, Colne supported by Cast
25 August	King Tut's Wah Wah Hut, Glasgow
28 August	Reading Festival
14 September	Boardwalk, Manchester

1993

19 January	Felix Club Sittard
27 January	Debra Murrell's House, Hounslow
15 April	Cardiff University
29 April	Loughborough University
5 May	The Wheatsheaf, Stoke
6 May	De Monfort University Leicester
7 May	University of Central England, Birmingham
8 May	Wedgewood Rooms, Portsmouth
9 May	The Wherehouse Derby
11 May	The Sugarhouse, Lancaster
12 May	King Tut's Wah Wah Hut, Glasgow
13 May	Riverside Newcastle
14 May	Bradford University
17 May	The Underworld, Camden
18 May	Manchester University
20 May	The Krazy, Liverpool
21 May	Fleece and Firkin, Bristol
24 June	Burnley Mechanics
4 August	Buzz Club, Chorlton
5 August	Duchess of York, Leeds
21 August	Heineken Music Festival, Southsea
4 October	Leeds University
5 October	Brunel University, London
7 October	Warwick University
8 October	Leicester University

9 October	Hothouse, Bournemouth
12 October	Wedgewood Rooms, Portsmouth
14 October	Manchester Academy 3 supported by Oasis
15 October	King Tut's Wah Wah Hut, Glasgow
19 October	Keele University, Stoke
20 October	The Borderline, Soho
21 October	Priory Social Club, Taunton
22 October	University of Sussex, Brighton
23 October	University of Central England, Birmingham
27 October	The Cavern, Exeter
28 October	Fleece and Firkin, Bristol
29 October	Derby University
30 October	University of East Anglia, Norwich

1994

20 January	Arena Amsterdam
21 January	Paard van Troje, The Hague
22 January	Club Niewe Pul Uden
7 May	The Carlton, Morecambe
2 June	Rock Garden, Covent Garden (Kingsize Screamer)
30 November	Rock Garden, Covent Garden (Kingsize Screamer)

1995

14 March	The Goodnight Club, Nelson (Kingsize Screamer) supported by The Cosmos
17 March	The Falcon, Camden (Kingsize Screamer)
23 March	The Borderline, Soho (Kingsize Screamer)
20 April	The Borderline, Soho (Kingsize Screamer)
14 October	The Monarch, Camden (Junkie)
13 November	The Falcon, Camden (Junkie)
November	Canterbury

1997

8 August	Burnley Mechanics
22 October	The Borderline, Soho

Nigel Wood

1998

2 July	Mean Fiddler, Harlesden
15 July	Camden Falcon
1 August	Queens Park, Burnley
17 October	Camden Falcon

1999

1 July	Pier Club, Brighton (Milo)
13 August	Sound Republic, Soho (Milo)
17 August	The Garage, Highbury (Milo)
7 September	The Garage, Highbury (Milo)
4 October	Hope & Anchor, Islington (Milo)
20 October	The Red Eye, Islington (Milo)
12 November	The Water Rats, King's Cross (Milo)
1 December	The Fallout Shelter, Soho (Milo)
14 December	The Borderline, Soho (Milo)

2000

9 February	The Social, Soho (Milo)
13 April	The Water Rats, King's Cross (Milo)

2002

22 February	Burnley Mechanics

2003

4 April	Burnley Mechanics

2004

23 July	Manchester Roadhouse
July	The Borderline, Soho
July	Kings Street Tavern, Accrington
July	Derby Arms, Colne

2012

4 November	The Muni, Colne

2015

25 April	The Fanzone at Turf Moor, Burnley
23 May	Gigantic Festival, Manchester Academy 2
6 November	Shiiine On, Butlins Minehead

2023

26 August	Trades Club, Hebden Bridge
25 November	Kanteena, Lancaster
23 December	Barnoldswick

2024

3 May	St Mary's Chambers, Rawtenstall
13 October	Lancaster Music Festival
17 November	Shiiine On, Butlin's Minehead
30 November	The Lexington, Islington
2 December	Barnoldswick Music & Arts Centre
3 December	Barnoldswick Music & Arts Centre

2025

9 May	100 Club, Oxford Street, London
24 May	The Trades, Hebden Bridge
25 May	Tim Burgess' Merch Market, Gorilla, Manchester
29 and 30 August	Music and Arts Centre, Barnoldswick
12 September	Stereo, Glasgow
19 September	Mercury Rising Festival, Stockport, Greater Manchester
5 December	The Muni, Colne

TV and Radio

May 1990
Granada Reports: Liverpool
'Seems to Me'

20 October 1990
Radio 1's *The Evening Session* with Nicky Campbell
'Something Cheap', 'Real', 'Sandman', 'Nationality'

3 December 1990
Radio 1's *The Evening Session* with Mark Goodier
'Which Way Should I Jump?', 'When it Comes', 'Here I Stand', 'Sally Ann'

Nigel Wood

1 February 1991
BBC1 *Blue Peter* with John Leslie
'Which Way Should I Jump?'
…and Blue Peter badges all around

5 February 1991
Greater London Radio (GLR), session with Gary Crowley
'Sally Ann', 'Here I Stand'

6 February 1991
BBC1 *Wogan*
'Which Way Should I Jump?'

16 February 1991
BBC1 *Going Live!* with Phillip Schofield
'Which Way Should I Jump?'

2 April 1991
2 Meter Sessions, Amsterdam
'Sally Ann', 'Rosemary Page', 'Here I Stand', 'Which Way Should I Jump?', 'Savage Earth Heart'

April 1991
On The Edge radio sessions, USA
'Rosemary Page'. 'Sally Ann'

9 June 1991
Radio Netherlands, Hilversum
'Here I Stand', 'Apple Green'

12 June 1991
Radio Netherlands, Hilversum
Live from Effenaar, Eindhoven

20 June 1991
France Inter, with Bernard Lenoir
'Sally Ann', 'Can't Find the Time', 'Savage Earth Heart', 'Spring Fever'
… and the interview in French with Simon

22 June 1991
Radio Switzerland
Live from Dolca Vita, Lausanne

June1991
Granada Reports: Liverpool
'Apple Green'

10 July 1991
BBC1 *Wogan*
'Apple Green'

21 April 1993
Radio 5 *Hit The North* with Mark Radcliffe
'Killing All The Good Men, Jimmy', 'Turn Off', 'Sleepwalking', 'Turn Me Over'

18 May 1993
GLR, with Gary Crowley
'Cool Breeze', 'Sweet Nothing'

8 July 1993
GLR, with Gary Crowley
'Positively 4th Street', 'Here I Stand'

23 August 1993
Radio 1 with Simon Campbell
'Pictures (Round My Room)', 'Killing All The Good Men, Jimmy', 'Turn Off', 'It's All Over Now, Baby Blue'

September 1993
Radio Forth, Edinburgh
'Cool Breeze', 'Career'

29 July 2004
Radio 6 Music, with Gideon Coe
'Sally Ann', 'When A Heart Stops Bleeding'

Nigel Wood

Albums

1991
Slinky (A&M Records)
More Slinky (A&M Records Japan only)

1993
Valve (A&M Records)

2004
Rubberband (Rubber Band Records)

2015
Long Road (Stanley Records)

2020
Stockholm (self-released)

2025
Boogie Woogie (Last Night From Glasgow)

Compilation Albums

1997
The Best Of Milltown Brothers (Spectrum Music)

2009
Best Of (Cherry Red Records)

2023
Tongue-Tied Mesmerised (Independent Singles and Demos 1987–1990) (Cherry Red Records)

Singles

1989
'Coming From The Mill' EP, 'Roses', 'Something On My Mind', We've Got Time' (Big Round Records)
'Which Way Should I Jump?' (Big Round Records)

1990
'Seems To Me', (Suburban)
'Apple Green', (A&M Records)

1991
'Which Way Should I Jump?' (A&M Records)

1993
'Turn Off' (A&M Records)
'It's All Over Now Baby Blue' (A&M Records)
'Sleepwalking' (A&M Records)

2015
'Long Road' (Stanley Records)

2020
'F.I.L.A.' (self-released)

2025
'Grab The Sun' (Last Night From Glasgow)

BIG THANKS

Along with the narratives of our lives kindly bringing us all here, the members of the band – Simon, Matthew, James, Nian and Barney – along with Mark Nelson, Jonathan Bibby, Nick Morrell, Max Elliott, Caroline Elleray, Steve Lamacq, Tim Paton, Nobby Hopkinson, Andy Devanney, Debbie Murrell, Stephen Rigg, Craig Eccles, and Laurence Hoare have been instrumental in the creation of this story. Nick and Max in particular deserve a little more than the briefest mentions in the book.

Nick was there. He's known most of the band for a long time. From primary school football teams and grammar school friends via dogsbody, gear shifter, roadie and hardcore fan, to James being best man at his wedding and Nian godparent to Nick's youngest child and only daughter.

You couldn't meet a more down-to-earth, honest, straight-forward bloke. He left Lancaster Grammar at 16 – yes, some people did, studied meat technology at Blackpool College because his mum and dad wouldn't sign his papers to go in the army, then went in the army for 10 years, then spent 24 years in the prison service. Consequently, he's the best subjective-objective control you could wish for.

'What can be better than watching your best mates playing brilliant indie rock music that's bursting with raw emotion and energy, everyone loving it and just seeing it get bigger and bigger?'

He attended the Spire's first gig at the Gregson Centre in May 1986. He loved it. Thereafter he just tagged along to anything he could and tried to help. For years. The Milltown Brothers were even responsible for him meeting Paula, his wife of 30 years. She was about to leave a party his sister was having at the family home while their mum and dad were away when

Nick, who had driven the band down to support Katrina and the Waves, eventually arrived home. Paula already had her coat on when he bumped into her walking in the door and said hello, at 3 o'clock in the morning.

Max was there even earlier. He was in the same class as Nian at primary school and was then in the same class as James, Nian, Nick and Matthew at Lancaster Grammar. Together with Nick they were the music-loving support gang. Roadies, cheerleaders, merchandise sellers and whatever for both the Spire and the Milltown Brothers – for the first few years of the bands' existence. After a few years Max quietly drifted away from the band. But this is the genesis of the Milltown Brothers, and Max is a good guy with a real talent for words, which he put to good use a few years later for James on one of his later projects, the Girl El Paranzo.

ABOUT THE AUTHOR

Nigel was born in Keighley in 1960. After surviving the perils of being the son of a policeman who was himself the son of a miner, and being in the frontline when Goole Grammar School united with Goole High School and became comprehensive in his third year, Nigel graduated from Leeds University in English Literature and Art History in 1982. Having resisted his dad's overtures to join the police, he spent his working life in a number of jobs based on an ability to write and appreciation of art and design. This began in 1984 writing holiday brochures in a bus station in Dewsbury and ended in 2011 as Creative Director of a branding and marketing business based in Sheffield which, in its most enjoyable phase, was called Dig For Fire, after the Pixies song. He went on to write and self-publish a novel *Is Poetry A Sport?* and run his own branding and creative consultancy Nothing But The Truth, a deliberate response to his former roles. Before beginning to research *And Jesus Danced (Twice)* in November 2023, he spent six years as a driftwood sculptor. He was happily married from 1985 to 2017 and has two sons, Jake and Joe. He describes himself as an existentialist, luck obsessive and wabi-sabi enthusiast.